Life UNSTUCK

Life UNSTUCK

Finding PEACE with Your Past,
PURPOSE in Your Present,
PASSION for Your Future

Pat Layton

Revell

a division of Baker Publishing Group
Grand Rapids, Michigan

Published by Revell
a division of Baker Publishing Group
P.O. Box 6287, Grand Rapids, MI 49516-6287
www.revellbooks.com

Printed in the United States of America

Library of Congress Cataloging-in-Publication Data is on file at the Library of Congress, Washington, DC.

ISBN 978-0-8007-2638-6

15 16 17 18 19 20 21   7 6 5 4 3 2 1

For the woman
who secretly suspects
there is nothing more
but desperately dreams there is.

Contents

Contents

Introduction

If I want to make my youngest grandkids laugh until sweet tea spews from their little noses, I remind them of the time we went tubing in the North Georgia Mountains. They love reliving the day we all piled into their mamma's SUV and trekked over to the rafting hut. We piled into four large black tubes with life jackets the size of Mini Coopers and divided three little ones amongst four adults. The water was high and flowing pretty gently. We were all excited for the "about three hours" we were about to enjoy on the chilly mountain river. We were not thirty minutes into that journey when Pop (what the grandbabies call my honey) found himself lifted up out of the flowing river and stuck up on a slippery rock. We all grabbed low-lying tree limbs to wait up while he and little Bella (who had immediately chosen him as her tube driver), jiggled back and forth as if on a see-saw until they finally slipped loose and rejoined us on the water. It was all good fun—until ten minutes later, when Pop was stuck again. Again, we all waited for him and Bella to dance a tube dance that set them free. We were enjoying lots of family laughs and fun teasing of Pop and Bella.

The bad news was this little delay in our "just long enough" journey over the river and through the woods kept happening over and over again. The sun was quickly slipping behind the trees and we were getting cold. Pop and Bella were getting wetter as they always seemed to be the ones in the water. It wasn't long before Pop began to lose his laugh and Bella started to cry and ask to move over to "G's tube." We ended up on the river for close to six hours with either Pop or one of the other adult tube-tenders stuck between scary rocks as the pace of the river became faster and more difficult to navigate. By the time we finally made our way to safety, we were all completely undone. The babies were blue with cold and the adults were exhausted from comforting them and questionably assuring them, "We *will* get unstuck and it will all be OK!"

●●●●●

I recently tested my unstuck theory on my Facebook family and was absolutely convinced by their responses that I was on the right track with my thoughts about all of this. They responded in the largest numbers I have ever received on my Facebook page. Relationships, finances, marriage, ministry, and on and on went the list. I can relate to every single stuck place my sisters shared. I have been in each one at some point or another, some even now.

As we take a look into life unstuck, we will be walking through a precious chapter in the Bible that most of us are fairly familiar with at least a few of the lines of, Psalm 139. I have lived the message of Psalm 139 on a daily basis for almost thirty years, since I started my own personal search for the freedom found in being unstuck, through its twenty-four life-changing verses.

I have discovered it is really easy to get *stuck*. Not so easy to get unstuck!

Sometimes it's our past that hangs us up and keeps us from flowing freely. Sometimes it's relationships that just don't seem to get better. You find you can't live with them and you can't live without them— you are stuck. Then there are those times when it's not "somebody else" that is keeping you trapped, it's *you*. Just you. Sometimes it's our own personal habits, lack of discipline, dead dreams, unmet expectations, lack of direction, or just plain old fear of trying.

The journey I travel in pursuit of a life unstuck is not unique to me. It is a journey and a destination God wants for all of His daughters. Our freedom is the reason Jesus surrendered His life on the cross. This amazing gift, alone, should inspire in our lives the passionate pursuit of every morsel of freedom's fruit. This truth should motivate us to do all we can to get unstuck and enjoy the journey of our lives.

In John 10:10, Jesus tells us He came so that you and I might have "life and have it abundantly" (ESV).

What does this mean? What does abundant life really look like?

How much freedom can we expect on this earth?

Just how unstuck should I expect to be . . . really?

You and I will answer these questions as we take this journey together. But before we begin, there is one central message I want us to grab right now and haul with us throughout this entire book. It must deeply penetrate our souls so that no enemy, circumstance, person, or thing can steal it. Ready?

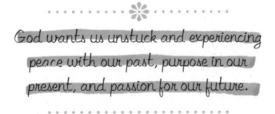

God wants us unstuck and experiencing peace with our past, purpose in our present, and passion for our future.

God wants us, His precious daughters, to be reminded and refreshed by the complete and unshakable knowledge of our redeemed life. He wants us completely restored from things that keep us stuck in the past and He wants us *set free* to gleefully anticipate all He has planned for our future.

Using six verses at a time from Psalm 139, this book will lay out a clear plan for every woman who senses there may be something missing, something hidden, or something unspeakable keeping her from fully experiencing the freedom and adventure promised by Jesus. This book is for the woman who secretly suspects there is nothing more but desperately dreams there is!

The truth is, we cannot experience an unstuck present if we have not truly dealt with our stuck past. You might just get to where you feel your past is unstuck, but guess what? Tomorrow—*today*—will be your past! We are a work in progress. I encourage you to take this journey one step at a time and really allow God to do a new thing in your heart and your life through His anointing upon these pages as He has done for me as I write. With that freedom, the best days of your life unstuck begin.

●●●●●

Before we get started, I want to pull your attention to the little "Unstuck Manifesto" that follows. I created this for us to claim together. I wrote it one day during the process of writing this book as I was basically lying on the floor crying to God, "I cannot do this! I cannot write anything worth reading. I am stuck! Stuck! Stuck!" One of my prayer partners told me right in the middle of my pity party, "Pat, get off the floor and just write. This is an attack. God's got this!"

Hmm . . . that sounds good. I'll just write that.

So, since I knew I would have at least *one* more pity party, either before the book was finished or after, I wrote this manifesto for myself, and prayerfully for you, my sister. Please flag the page it's on and say it before every chapter, together with a book buddy, after you finish the book, or any time you need to be reminded of its truths.

From me to you.

For a free downloadable study guide and additional resources for each chapter, visit life-unstuck.com.

UNSTUCK
Manifesto

I declare in the name of the Lord Jesus Christ that today my life is filled with peace with the past, purpose in the present, and passion for the future. I am unstuck and free! I declare that no weapon formed against me shall prosper and that my weapons have divine power to destroy arguments and take every thought captive that does not proclaim the victory of Jesus in my life. I will not give in to fear of any kind: fear of the past, fear of the present, or fear of the future. I am blessed to be a blessing until my assignment on this earth has been completed and I am standing face-to-face with my Jesus, celebrating His completed and perfect work in me. **I am unstuck!**

I will waste no opportunity to glorify my God and to share His great plan for me and for all mankind. I will waste no opportunity to experience the anointing He has placed on my life. I will embrace every opportunity He places in my life. I will not accept a trace of apathy in my attitude. I declare abundance in my marriage, my family, my life, and my ministry. I have the Holy Spirit as my guide, my comforter, and my power. I have stepped over the line into God's good grace and will never, ever turn back, slow down, back away, be quiet, or let up. I am a woman of God and a disciple of Jesus Christ. **I am unstuck!**

My past is redeemed, my present is hemmed in, and my future is secure. I am done with low living, sight walking, small plans, smooth knees, colorless dreams, tamed visions, worldly measures, faithless talk, and little goals. I love and live by faith, lavish grace on others, lean on His presence, walk in patience, am undergirded and uplifted by prayer, and am strengthened by power. My face is set, my walk is steady, my goal is heaven, my road is narrow, my Guide is faithful, and my mission is clear. I will not be compromised, bought, detoured, lured away, turned back, deluded, or delayed. I will not flinch in the face of sacrifice, hesitate in the presence of adversity, negotiate at the table of the enemy, meander in the maze of mediocrity, or ponder at the pool of popularity. **I am unstuck!**

I determine to stay prayed up, preached up, stored up, and praised up. I have been given the power to change and the power to make good choices. I can love myself and I can love others. I am secure and surrounded by God's love. I am unstuck from fear, unstuck from shame, unstuck from mediocrity, and unstuck from insecurity. My battle is not against flesh and blood but against a weak, stupid, uncreative, and defeated enemy who fights me because he fears me. I will stand my ground and fight any lie he places in front of me. I will dismantle every argument with the piercing power of God's Word. Every time he reminds me of my past, I will remind him of his future. **I am unstuck!**

I will stand under the impenetrable covering of the blood of Jesus—for greater is He who is in me than he who is in the world. I can do all things through Him. Though my enemy surrounds me, God surrounds my enemy. My God has all authority over my life. He is my God, the Creator of the heavens and the earth. He is the supreme Author of all existence and rules and reigns over my life. In Him all things exist. He is my Lord, my Master, and my Owner. He is holy and will watch over and teach me all things. He will direct me in the way I should go. He will never leave me nor forsake me. His peace is mine. His provision is mine. His love is mine. His hope is mine. His passion is mine. He is my Comforter, Counselor, and Friend.

I choose this day to live an unstuck life. **I am unstuck!**

Section One

Just Imagine
Life Unstuck

Psalm 139:1–6

You have searched me, LORD,
  and you know me.
You know when I sit and when I rise;
  you perceive my thoughts from afar.
You discern my going out and my lying down;
  you are familiar with all my ways.
Before a word is on my tongue
  you, LORD, know it completely.
You hem me in behind and before,
  and you lay your hand upon me.
Such knowledge is too wonderful for me,
  too lofty for me to attain.

1

UNSTUCK
Possibilities

You have searched me, LORD, and you know me.

Psalm 139:1

Getting Naked

Do I want to live or do I want to die?
   I'm thinking die.
   Right now.

As I struggled to open my eyes, I was only aware of one thing—
my freezing cold, naked *bottom* was sticking up in the air, surrounded by chattering voices.

As my eyes began to slowly focus, the first thing I saw was Dr.
Kildaire (think Patrick Dempsey on steroids). He was leaning over
me, wiping my brow with a washcloth. Some of those chattering
people were indeed looking at my naked rear end, while others

acted as if it wasn't even sticking up and *exposed* for the whole world to see—and, believe me, it most definitely was. At that precise moment I realized a life-changing truth: exposure can be very uncomfortable.

As I slowly regained consciousness, the events of the past twenty-four hours began to quickly return to my mind, and I saw my husband's face at the back of the crowd, straining to see what all the commotion was about. I remembered I was on a cruise ship. My husband and I had been enjoying the better part of a week on this fabulous ship with my three sisters and their husbands. My parents, nowhere near wealthy, had surprised us with a once-in-a-lifetime trip for Christmas: a five-day cruise to the glorious Bahamas. Not only that, but they had given us the added blessing of watching all eight grandchildren so all four sisters and our husbands could go together. From the moment we got in the car to go to Miami, we were 100 percent *giddy.* The ship, aglow with lights and luxury, was a dream. The lounge chairs and tall skinny drinks with umbrellas available every day were a dream. Adorning ourselves in fancy dresses at night and spending long sunny days snorkeling in tropical reefs was like a dream. There was not a juice box to be seen, anywhere, and having no one pressing up under my back when I woke up in the morning (well, no *little* person anyway) was beyond any dream possible.

But now? *Oh my.*

Right there in those moments, my beautiful dream quickly turned into a nightmare.

Yes, exposure can be *very* uncomfortable.

You see, on the last day of our adventure, heading back toward the reality of home and the responsibilities of parenting, we overheard the crew murmuring softly of inclement weather ahead. Although they assured the passengers it was nothing to worry about, they did tell us all we might want to retire to our cabins early that evening with some Dramamine to get us through the "slightly turbulent" night. We were told the ship would be secure in port when we awoke.

That was the plan.

That plan was *not* reality.

Sometimes my plans for my life and the realities of actual life forget to communicate.

Needless to say, this was one of those times. After eating a very wobbly "last supper" on the cruise ship, we all took the captain's advice and headed to bed early. That was the good news. The bad news was that January storm was far worse than the crew expected. This one-hundred-thousand-ton ship hit one of Florida's worst-recorded winter storms head-on. The wave swells were over forty feet and tossed that huge vessel around the Caribbean like a beach ball. In the midst of those swells I woke up being literally thrown across the cabin. *Smack!* Those waves tossed me from one side of our tiny cabin to the other, but that was nothing compared to what was transpiring *inside* my body. *Seasick* is not a big enough word to describe the violent retching and heaving I was doing. I literally was not able to stand up.

Little did I know that night would become one of our big marriage stories. I called out to my "knight in shining armor" for help, only to be told he didn't want to move because he was afraid *he* would get sick. Oh boy. You can imagine how *that* story has been used over the past thirty-seven years. It's one of my favorite stories to recount to tease my husband.

After an indeterminable amount of time, I was finally able to get to the door of our cabin on my hands and knees. I was desperate for just a small wisp of fresh air, but when I opened the door from our cabin, I was horrified. There before me in the tiny hallway was most of the ship's crew, all on the floor, all vomiting.

This was not good.

What happened next became a bit of a blank. I remember somehow working my way up a few flights of stairs to get to an open deck only to have the wind be so strong I could not get the door completely open. It was then that everything went blank. Sometime during the night I must have managed to find Dr. Kildaire, who gave me a shot of "yum-yum" that knocked me out and landed me with my naked bottom sky-up in the midst of a crowd of strangers.

> You have searched me, LORD,
> and you know me. (Ps. 139:1)

So many things about this story come to my mind as I read these words.

Starting with the fact that I was searched up and down by Dr. Kildaire and not forgetting the rest of the strangers surrounding my bare bottom. In this nine-word verse, David is declaring a life-changing truth: God searches us and knows us.

God knows right here, right now, where your life is stuck *and* unstuck.

He sees our hearts and He searches our souls. He watches us move and He hears us talk. He knows what we think and He knows what we fear. God wants us to enjoy life unstuck in *every* way. He wants us to enjoy peace, purpose, and passion at every stage of life, but sometimes it doesn't seem that way. Sometimes I feel like everyone "gets it" but me. Sometimes I feel *stuck* in being completely unsatisfied with myself, wishing I was someone else, somewhere else, or doing something else. I often feel stuck in seeking affection or approval that is always just beyond my reach. Sometimes it's not the bad stuff that keeps me stuck—sometimes it's the secret dreams I have for life I can't bear to share for fear they might sound ridiculous or silly. Sometimes I feel like the masks I wear for everyone else are going to completely take over and I will disappear behind somebody I don't even know.

Sometimes exposure can be uncomfortable.

Then I read these words: God searches me and *knows* me. If God, the God of the universe, Creator of all life, knows all and sees all, then what do I have to lose by letting it all out and exposing who I really am—good, bad, and beautiful?

What do I have to lose by risking it all and getting naked, so to speak, before God and others to see what God really has inside of me?

The God Who Sees It All

In this very first verse, David is reminding himself of a truth about God he had learned from his childhood Hebrew lessons: one name for God is *El Roi*—the God Who Sees! With a sense of wonder in his words, David acknowledges that God sees everything, from the inside (his heart) to the outside (his actions).

God sees the good, the bad, and the ugly in each of us. As we take our first dip into the stunning beauty of Psalm 139, we discover what a personal God we serve. David has a confident relationship with God. In fact, God's thoughts are all about him, as far as David is concerned. The twenty-four intimate verses in this psalm use some version of the word *me* over forty times. No, David is not being conceited. What makes David different from most Christians today is that David admits and embraces the truth that God is always thinking about him. Likewise, God is always thinking about you. God knows what you are doing, what you are thinking, and what you ate for breakfast. He knows your fears and when and why you hide from everyone—including yourself.

Our brains have a difficult time wrapping around this reality, don't they? There have been many times in my life as a woman, a

23

wife, and a mom when I felt I *needed* to see everything, everywhere, all the time, but I just could not. I, just like you, am limited in my abilities. However, stepping into the amazing glory of Psalm 139, we are confronted right out of the gate with the reality that God has *already* searched us. He *already* knows us, which means all of us: our hearts, words, thoughts, actions, and intentions. This very thought that the God of the universe, my Creator, my Savior, has seen what I have done has brought me tremendous peace, and sometimes lack of peace, many times in my life. Can you relate?

I have a not-so-pretty past. I have made some decisions not worthy of a holy God to watch. And honestly? I still do. The difference between then and now is that now my life is devoted to searching and knowing God right back.

> GOD, investigate my life;
>   get all the facts firsthand
> I'm an open book to you;
>   even from a distance, you know what I'm thinking.
>   (Ps. 139:1–2 Message)

> O Lord, you have examined my heart
>   and know everything about me. (v. 1 NLT)

The word *searched* used in this verse refers to investigating or exploring the earth by boring or digging in it. The literal interpretation of this word is "to search the earth for water or precious metals." It means to search accurately or closely. As a result of that close investigation, nothing is concealed. Everything is laid bare. *Everything.* Psalm 139:1 led me to the first truth about real freedom!

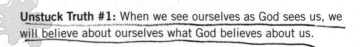

Unstuck Truth #1: When we see ourselves as God sees us, we will believe about ourselves what God believes about us.

3-D Women

As you may have guessed from my rather vulnerable story earlier, I grew up in a home with three sisters, in addition to a mom and a female dog named Missy. I have spent the past twenty-five years of my life in full-time women's ministry. My life has been spent among and shared with women. I have learned much about us girls: how we think, what we feel, how we respond, how we don't respond. My slightly "unscientific" conclusion is that we are truly 3-D women. My philosophy is that at any given moment we are either dizzy, desperate, or digging. Sometimes we accomplish all three in a day, sometimes all in the same minute, but I have decided that all women are 3-D. Don't believe me? I bet you the cost of this book that one or more of these "Ds" describes your life *right now.* .

> Dizzy: Dizzy women live life in a perpetual spin cycle. Juggling children, jobs, husbands, finances, laundry, errands, sports, balanced meals, bagged lunches, and so forth, dizzy women barely have enough time between when the alarm goes off in the morning to when they collapse into bed at night to hold things together, much less ponder what God thinks about them. Dizzy women search for unstuck peace.
>
> Desperate: Desperate women seek God with every fiber of their being: their heart, their emotions, their mind, their strength. Such women are in a place so intense, so painful, so seemingly hopeless that only God can rescue them. Only God can bring peace to desperate women. Only God can work the mess out. Desperate women search for unstuck hope.
>
> Digging: Digging women just want *more.* Digging women can be dizzy and they can even be desperate, but they are hungry for more. Digging women may secretly suspect there is nothing more, but desperately dream there is. More from God, more answers, more purpose . . . all leading to more questions

such as "What is next for me?" "Why am I here?" "Where do I serve?" "What do you want me to do, Lord?" Digging women search for unstuck answers.

So, was I right? Can you see yourself in at least one of those descriptions? Life can be very tough for us females. Womanhood is not an easy journey. We start out with the emotional trauma of water weight, mood swings, and puberty. We soon graduate to labor pains, baby blues, and back-talking teens, and eventually end girl world with hot flashes and empty nests. Through it all, I often feel the *opposite* of "searched" and "seen." I usually feel invisible, completely unnoticed, like my life is just a vapor of moving from one person's neediness to another. I often feel like everyone is too *dizzy*, *desperate*, and *digging* in their own lives to give a hoot about me. I often feel no one really "searches" me enough to know me. I have secrets, even now. Even from my best friends.

Be honest. Right now, I'll bet there is at least one thing in your heart or life you have not shared with your best friend, your husband, or even your mother. Am I right?

But the truth is God does search you and He does know you. He knows your secrets and He still loves you without exception. In fact, to God—it is all about *you*.

I can honestly say that I had never (until I dug deep into these verses of Scripture), *ever* uttered the words "It's all about *me*," unless it was a joke. I want you to just stop for a minute and say those words yourself, out loud.

Say it: "It's all about me."

Say it: "God is all about me!"

God is all about you!

Since I started offering my woman's conference, Imagine Me . . . Set Free, I have imagined the hair has stood up on the necks of a few ministry leaders when I coached the ladies to declare such "heresy." We are truly and faithfully taught it is not about us, "It is all about Jesus." Don't get me wrong, it definitely is all about Jesus, but what I want us to see in God's Word is how Jesus is *all about you*. He left the holiness of heaven *for you*. He left His Father *for you*. Jesus said,

> I have come that they may have life, and that they may have it more abundantly. (John 10:10 NKJV)

3-D God

Want some good news? The reason we all live as 3-D women is that you and I were created by and serve a 3-D God. He is not dizzy or desperate, but He is digging . . . for you! God used a pattern of Himself to create each one of us and we were fashioned after a three-dimensional God. At the same time, I think as women we sometimes need to be reminded that although we are created in God's image, we are *not* God. The Bible uses some big words to describe our big God.

He is omniscient (all-knowing). Psalm 139 reveals a God who knows everything, at all times, for all time. He is also a God who completely knows *you*. His knowledge is perfect, and nothing happening in your life, or done in your life, is hidden from Him. He knows your each and every thought, word, way, and movement.

He is omnipresent (ever-present). He is a God who is anywhere and everywhere all the time. He is in the kitchen and the bedroom; He is in the hospital room and the boardroom; He is in the carpool and the gym. God is with you no matter where you are. You can never be out of His sight or beyond His grip.

He is omnipotent (all-powerful). God is limitless in His power and is in complete control of all circumstances. God created and designed everything, including our minds, bodies, and spirits. Therefore, He has all authority over our hearts, minds, and wills. His *power* and *control* have no limits.

As women, we should be comforted knowing God's eyes are always upon us, but I know sometimes we are not so sure. There have been many times in my life when I was not so sure God could see me, and even times when I didn't want Him to see me. Yet when we are able to fully grasp the truth that God knows all our past, is keenly aware of our needs and is with us in the present, and holds every moment of our future, it is then we experience true freedom. *Remember: when we see ourselves as God sees us, we will believe about ourselves what God believes about us.*

The good news is that God sees our sin and our running. He also sees us as we are meant to be. He sees the beginning, the middle, and the end. He holds us right now! He is in control and has created us for His glory. If you will allow God to speak to you through Psalm 139, you will understand that life unstuck and real freedom begin with a 3-D God searching and knowing us as the 3-D women we are. We allow His 3-D to wrap around our 3-D, and we experience life unstuck. We begin to live the abundant and free life Jesus wants for us when and *only* when we see what God sees in us and embrace who we are to Him.

Come with me on this journey through what many people feel is the most beautiful and poetic chapter of the Bible. Let's get naked! Let's get unstuck! Stop the world and the worry in your heart, mind, and even your body, and allow this book, this journey, to be "all about you."

Let's allow ourselves to be searched and known—past, present, and future—by the One who truly *sees* us. To God, you are not invisible. You are not too broken, alone, or damaged to be seen

28

through His eyes. You have not messed up too badly and you are not too far from His grip to be wrapped up in His loving arms.

Ready? Take some time—I mean it, girl. Get some coffee, tea, or some grapes. Sit somewhere alone and let God get you started on this journey by taking the Unstuck Assessment you'll find on the next page. Think about your answers. Let yourself prepare to be amazed by God.

UNSTUCK
Assessment

*L*et's start with taking a look at where our life might be slipping toward—or maybe smack in the middle of—*stuck*. I am pretty sure there has been some time in your life, maybe even now, when you felt like you had just walked through some gum and your shoe was stuck to the floor. Haven't you discovered how the more you struggle against that yucky gum the nastier it gets? I have learned that the best way to get out of a mess like that is by taking a knife or other sharp object straight to the point of attack. That, my friend, is exactly the plan. But first, let's assess the situation, shall we?

Read the following statements, and next to each one I want you to place a number from one to five, one being, "I'm completely *unstuck* in this thought or experience and enjoy full victory through Christ here," and five being, "I am so *stuck* here, I feel imprisoned by this and need release with Christ's help."

1. I am afraid to let my Christian friends know about my real everyday struggles for fear of what they will think of me.
2. I often feel I can't get anything right.

30

3 3. I am stuck constantly comparing myself with others around me, and just never "measure up."

3 4. The failures of my past just never seem to go away.

3 5. There is nothing "special" about me. I have nothing "different" to offer.

5 6. It seems to me like everybody else I know is moving ahead in life and I am just *stuck*.

1 7. If I tell my kids about my past I will lose all their respect.

3 8. There are people I can never forgive for what they did to me.

3 9. I should have followed my dream years ago, but it's too late now. I missed my chance.

4 10. I don't think God really cares one way or the other what I do with my life.

3 11. I often feel judged.

5 12. If I were different (thinner, prettier, richer, smarter, older, younger . . .), I would see my dreams come true.

5 13. Fear is keeping me from doing something I have always wanted to do.

4 14. I have tried to change but I just can't. I have too many areas where I feel stuck. I have no idea where to start.

4 15. On a scale of 1–5, I feel stuck. (Remember, 1 is unstuck, 5 is totally stuck.)

Now, add up all your numbers, and see where you fall on our unstuck scale.

(0–15) You are in great unstuck shape. Way to go! Not only have you learned much of how to live your own life unstuck, you have the ability to share it with your sisters and the world. Thank you for picking up this book and joining my passion for life unstuck.

(16–20) You are on your way to unstuck living. Just look at where God has brought you thus far in your life. The great news is that He wants to continue your healing until *all* areas of your life are completely unstuck. Your victory is in sight!

(**21–50**) God is so good to you. He is using this book and this time in your life to show you where He wants to set you free and get you unstuck. Gently and lovingly, He will be showing you where there is a better way and giving you hope to fully grasp an unstuck and free life.

(**51+**) Your journey begins today. I am so proud of you for not only being honest with yourself but also believing there is something more, something so much better than what you have now. Remember, Jesus came to give *you* abundant life.

. . . .

Visit life-unstuck.com to become a member of the Unstuck Woman Club.

2

UNSTUCK
Thoughts

You know when I sit and when I rise; you perceive my thoughts from afar.

Psalm 139:2

From an airplane window on a sunny, clear day, no city on earth could be more beautiful than what you see when flying into Tampa International Airport. Sparkling like glitter, whitecaps rock happy boaters over aqua blue water that is so transparent and clear you swear you can see a blue crab on the sandy bottom from a thousand feet up. Because of our world-class Tampa Bay weather, more often than not the sky is so blue against the ocean that it is difficult to tell where one stops and the other begins. Were it not for the powdery white sand that separates the two dueling delights of God's creative awesomeness, it would all look like a breathtaking wall of blue.

Have I made you want to take a vacation? (Please let me know if you visit!) It sounds so mesmerizingly thrilling to watch, right? Wrong.

For me, it is a rare and treasured moment to be relaxed enough to enjoy the beauty of Tampa Bay from the sky. You see, I do *not* like to fly and am rarely relaxed enough to enjoy the view. In fact, when I surrendered my life to Jesus over thirty years ago, I made a bold announcement to Him (yep—I just said that) that I would do *anything* for Him and the kingdom of God *but* speak in front of crowds and fly on airplanes.

Dah, duh, duh, dah!

It's no real surprise that I have been speaking to crowds and flying on airplanes for about twenty-five years. I have learned to trust God in airplanes. I have reached a place where I refuse to let Satan keep me stuck in fear and steal my love for speaking and travel through fear of flying. Don't get me wrong. This is not an easy unstuck choice. I have had all the self-talks about the dangers of car driving versus flying. I have scanned the faces of other passengers to see who is on the plane that God would *never* let perish in a plane crash, such as the adorable (albeit loud) toddler sitting in front of me. I have read Scripture and listened to praise music, all the while soaking a tissue with my tears and praying the person sitting next to me didn't notice—but surely they did. I have traveled from one airport to another in a plane that was teasing the ground and traumatizing my tummy the entire flight to the point that, upon landing, I fell facedown on the airport floor and thanked Jesus for the ground. And, no, I am *not* kidding!

I clearly remember one flight I took with my daughter. The plane was in the throes of a winter snowstorm. I gripped the armrest and held my breath. My daughter? She slept peacefully. She always does that! So, what was the difference between my flight and hers?

We shared the same tiny old plane.

We shared the same hundred-mile-per-hour winds.

We shared the same roller-coaster ride.

We faced death together.

The difference was our *thoughts*! My daughter was not thinking *death, crash and burn, no goodbye notes*. No, she was thinking differently.

Unstuck women think differently.

Unstuck women tap into what is *good* and think on that.

Unstuck women follow faith.

Unstuck women look for the good in all circumstances.

Unstuck women bounce back from failure.

Unstuck women face challenges differently.

The truth is that if I want life unstuck, I have to *think* unstuck. You see, who we are, what we do, how we behave, and what we say all generate from deep inside of us, a process that starts in the heart and comes to life in a thought.

What Was I Thinking?

The heart always represents—physically, spiritually, and emotionally—the very *center* of our being. It is the place where our actions, attitudes, beliefs, and *thoughts* all originate. Psalm 139:2 reminds us that God not only searches us and knows us, He knows us *intimately* and He knows us *inside out*. Do you remember the first truth we shared? When we see ourselves as God sees us, we will believe about ourselves what God believes about us.

It all starts in the heart! You cannot change your thoughts until you let God change your heart. God created me, and you, from the inside out. God knows us this way: our inside life (*thought*) defines our outside life (*action*). Everything begins in the heart. Look at this verse of Scripture that reminds us how our thoughts matter to God.

> For the word of God is alive and active. Sharper than any double-edged sword, it penetrates even to dividing soul and spirit, joints and marrow; it judges the thoughts and attitudes of the heart. (Heb. 4:12)

Priscilla Shirer, in her book *The Resolution for Women*, says it this way:

> The heart is the reservoir, and a holding tank for every attitude and belief we've either placed there or allowed to hang out there. It is the storehouse containing the essence of who we are—and because of its direct link to our ongoing habits and actions—the picture of who we are becoming.[1]

Our thoughts are the vessel or tool used to get what is in the heart *out* of the heart. So, what are thoughts, exactly? Thoughts can be a single idea or an arrangement of ideas. They can be the product of thinking or mental activity, a consideration or reflection of an idea. Thoughts can even be explained using emotional words such as *anticipation*, *consideration*, *care*, and *belief*. Thoughts are studied and researched in any number of scientific fields too, such as biology, psychology, sociology, anthropology . . . wow! Although there is no generally accepted agreement as to how they form, everyone agrees that thoughts are a fundamental human activity, take place in the brain, are a part of a biological system, and happen consciously.

Our family had a goldfish pond in our backyard for many years. We loved to feed our fish and watch them grow into all sorts of magnificent colors. During the winter, as the weather turned chilly, the goldfish always found some sort of depth to that pond we never knew existed to stay warm. No matter how hard we tried to find them, when the cold hit they disappeared. Then, when we felt as though they could not have survived the chilly water, sure enough when the warm days of spring came, out popped those goldfish.

Our hearts are similar to that goldfish pond. Our hearts happily show off our colors, our joy, and the nourishment given to us from our communities, but when adversity hits we withdraw and retreat into the deepest part of ourselves, and hide until it is safe to resurface. In those depths, what is found? When we are left with nothing but our thoughts and our heart's cry, are the words true or are they lies? I think we can all agree that our thought life is powerful, for good and for bad. I also think we can agree that our thought life is complex. As we begin to take a look at all its complexities, I think it is foundational for us to first consider the *condition* of our hearts where all thought is born.

Four Facts about Getting Unstuck

1. Getting Unstuck Starts in the Heart

The heart is the key for life unstuck. The Bible is full of words and directions for the heart. God obviously sees the outside. Psalm 139:2 starts with the words "You know when I sit and when I rise." People notice when we sit and when we get up; they notice our actions, our speech, and our behaviors. But unlike people, God can also see what we have on the inside. He knows that what is hidden in our hearts will eventually lead to what we think and what is acted out in our lives.

> The good [woman] out of the good treasure of [her] heart brings forth what is good; and the evil [woman] out of the evil treasure brings forth what is evil. (Luke 6:45 NASB)

2. Getting Stuck Starts in the Head

The enemy has no weapon when you are watching your heart as God directs. His first place of attack is what you think and believe about yourself, what you think and believe others think of you, and what you think and believe about God. If the devil can plant doubt, discouragement, fear, or unbelief into your thought life, he's got you where he wants you. He is the "father of lies," as God's Word states in John 8:44, so the last thing he wants is for you to truly consider what is in your heart, much less to see if it aligns with truth and think differently! Remember, unstuck women *think* differently.

> Watch over your heart with all diligence,
> For from it flow the springs of life. (Prov. 4:23 NASB)

3. Life Unstuck Starts in the Heart and Comes to Life in the Head

It all starts in the heart. Jesus didn't die just to give you eternal life beginning when you leave this world and enter into heaven; He died to bring you freedom and abundant life *now*. Jesus died for you to live life unstuck. At the same time, God gives us what is called *free will*. In order to allow God to change our hearts, we have to choose to fill our heads with His truth. We have to read, study, say, and pray God's Word. When we intentionally choose to believe God's Word, it sinks from the head to the heart and changes us. God's Word changes our hearts. No work. No worries.

> It is for freedom that Christ has set us free. Stand firm, then, and do not let yourselves be burdened again by a yoke of slavery. (Gal. 5:1)

Oswald Chambers says it this way:

> It is accomplished through a series of moral choices. God does not make us holy in the sense that He makes our character holy. He

makes us holy in the sense that he made us innocent before Him. And then we have to turn that innocence into holy character through the moral choices we make.[2]

Just as without a heartbeat there is no life, without a healthy heart there is no good thinking. If your heart is not healthy, your thoughts will not be healthy, and nothing will be healthy in your life. You will live stuck in stinking thinking.

> For as [she] thinks in [her] heart, so is [she].
> (Prov. 23:7 NKJV)

It's a cycle for life unstuck. Thoughts result in beliefs, and beliefs lead to life—stuck or unstuck. We all have stuck thinking from time to time; it comes with being a human being. God says He can *change* the way we think if we will think like He thinks. When we give God permission to change our thinking and renew our minds with His truth, He will by His Holy Spirit prompt our hearts to be responsive to His way of thinking, which will have a life-changing, unstuck effect on the rest of our lives.

4. God Is Watching You—Inside and Out!

In Psalm 139, David is saturated in the reality of God's "all-seeing eye." The story of David starts in 1 Samuel 16 and comes to a close of sorts in 1 Kings 2:10. It is a fascinating story and worthy of being read in its entirety. I wish we had time to dig more into David's full story, but many other great studies have accomplished that far better than I ever could. However, it is interesting to note that when David was first chosen from among Jesse's sons, God spoke these words to the prophet Samuel:

> Do not consider his appearance or his height. . . . The LORD does not look at the things people look at. People look at the outward appearance, but the LORD looks at the heart. (1 Sam. 16:7)

How God Thinks

If we know how the freedom and abundant life we crave hinge upon our thoughts, what are our next steps? How do we do this "thinking like God thinks" thing? One step at a time, one minute at a time, one hour at a time, one day at a time. Remember:

> For as [she] thinks in [her] heart, so is [she].
> (Prov. 23:7 NKJV)

Where the thoughts go, the woman goes. We are led down our paths in life guided, literally, by our thoughts. OK, we've got that, right? The next thing is really, really simple: we think what God thinks. But how? How do we think what God thinks? Aren't His ways and His thoughts higher than ours? How can we possibly think like the Almighty thinks? Again, it is really simple. We fill our minds with God's Word.

Unstuck Truth #2: If we want to see what God sees, we have to think like God thinks.

Ponder with me a bit on God's Word. Our lives are led by our thoughts, which originate within our hearts and come out through our mouths. It's the same way with God! His heart is good and perfect and holy. This holy and wholly wonderful heart leads Him to think marvelous and tender thoughts toward *you*. And His Word has power. It was by the very Word of God that the stars were flung into place, the waters separated to form land, and our punishment for sin was *finished*. God's Word has power! God's Word can, therefore, powerfully change you and your thoughts.

> Do not conform to the pattern of this world, but be transformed by the renewing of your mind. Then you will be able to test and approve what God's will is—his good, pleasing and perfect will. (Rom. 12:2)

Simply put, we roll God's Word over and over in our minds until we start to think what He thinks. When we replace our natural thoughts with God's *supernatural* thoughts, we replace lies with truth—and truth sets us free; truth gets us unstuck.

Once we know God's Word about us, we will live victoriously in the freedom God so freely offers us. Don't fret; it is difficult at first. Bad habits are always difficult to break, and retraining your patterns, your beliefs, and your ways will take time and practice but will lead to great freedom and joy. Is that not worth the time to apply God's Word to laying a firm foundation, one that will last, one that will endure? Sure it is! So take command over your thoughts through the Word of God and kick the enemy right on out. Demand that insecurity no longer has any place in your life. Line your thoughts up with God's promises and let those good and true and beautiful words give you lasting joy, enduring peace, and get you unstuck. You can do this because you are worth it and God is *all about you.*

3

UNSTUCK
Personality

You discern my going out and my lying down; you are familiar with all my ways.

Psalm 139:3

S orry, ma'am, but you are overweight."

My head shot up. "Excuse me?"

I was attempting to reposition my rolling carry-on suitcase. I was struggling to keep it from flipping on its side, again, for the fourteenth time since dragging it out of my car, and I was not succeeding. *He did not just say what I think he said, did he?*

"You are overweight."

Yep, he said it. My brain began to rush into a riot of responses, and I thought, *I knew I should have skipped that banana pudding milkshake yesterday.*

"Your suitcase, ma'am? Your suitcase is overweight."

"Ohhhh!" *Praise the Lord.* "I can fix that. No problem."

I quickly reorganized things and was on my way, now allowing myself to eat more than celery and cucumbers for the next month.

I travel a lot these days. After I spent over twenty years leading a large pregnancy resource center ministry in Tampa, Florida, God hauled me out of my comfort zone and flung me into the air. A new adventure of speaking and writing has put me on close to five hundred airplanes over the past few years. How do I know this? Because every single airplane I step on is a step of faith for me; as I shared in the last chapter, I absolutely do not like to fly! So you can see why traveling is one of my greatest challenges.

There isn't a single thing I like about air travel or airplanes, but the part I like least of all has to be the airport check-in process. When I think about what a few bad men (aka terrorists) have done to the process of getting on an airplane and traveling somewhere, well, it makes me steam a bit.

One of the responses to September 11 was the creation of that lovely X-ray screening part of getting through security. I refused being X-rayed for a long time until I realized having a strange woman run her hands up and down my inner thighs to places that invaded my personal space, albeit still my *outside* stuff, was far worse than having the entire security staff see my *inside* stuff. Not to mention the very obvious "Let's make the process miserable for anyone who refuses the X-ray screening" unwritten code of all airports in the nation. Oh, it still makes my blood boil a bit, but also chuckle.

One of the many results of all that flying is that although my husband knows me, my Mom knows me, my kids know me, and my friends know me, airport personnel know me best. Unlike anyone else but God, they have seen me inside and out!

● ● ● ● ●

God knew what He wanted to do through me, and He knew it would require me to depend fully on Him because He is *well acquainted* with my scaredy-cat ways on planes and in front of crowds.

Besides the personal fears I struggle with, I have just a few other quirks and annoying habits. For example, whenever I am sitting down, whether it is in a rocking chair, a lawn chair, or a dentist's chair—I shake my foot. Once my husband and I were at a movie when the person beside me gently nudged me and asked, very politely, mind you, "Would you please stop shaking your foot?" I was so embarrassed. I realized I had been so involved in the intensity of the movie that I hadn't noticed the six people to my left leaning over and watching, with annoyance, my foot going a hundred miles per hour. The entire row of chairs was shaking! I have done this for as long as I can remember. I have been teased about it as long as I can remember too.

How about another example from my life, say, my daughter? I still remember the first thing I noticed about her . . . her lips. It was pretty unbelievable really, to focus on lips, all things considered. After all, she was only ten inches long for heaven's sake! My wedding ring could have slipped over her tiny arm. A teeny, tiny baby covered with fine silky hair, a protection babies carry right up until birth. However, her birth was early—very, very early. I'll tell you more about her later. Her body, not knowing it had been born prematurely, still protected itself. She was the size of a tiny baby squirrel but she had the most amazing lips! They were deep pink and perfectly shaped the way lips are supposed to be. Full and round across the top with a perfect deep dip in the middle to create definition and reflect her sweet, peaceful mood.

That was twenty-five years ago.

Today, that daughter of mine still has those adorable lips, but what she does not seem to ever have enough of is lipstick. Let me correct that: she never seems to have enough of *any* makeup. She always, I repeat *always*, has to steal (I mean borrow) mine! It's not that she doesn't actually *have* her own makeup, she just never knows where *her* makeup is. I, on the other hand, practically have my makeup alphabetized so she always knows where to find it when she needs it.

Being her mamma, I am well acquainted with my daughter's ways. She is sensitive, loyal, and tenderhearted. She is also sloppy, disorganized, and hmm . . . can I say it in a book? Yes, I can, I am the writer—she is *messy*. Messy! Messy! In all fairness, she would probably have just a few things to say about me, since she knows my ways too. Something like, "My mom is organized, energetic, and creative. She is also controlling, demanding, and *bossy*. Bossy!"

Yep, our family, just like yours, is a garden of personalities. Each member of our family, just like yours, has a unique personality and a particular propensity to "pain in the neck" behavior patterns that make the rest of us "normal people" go nuts. Being in families also gives us the unique position of being so familiar with each person's ways (pet peeves, hot-button issues, you get the idea) that we can almost guess what someone's particular reaction will be, right? And God, you see, is the same way: He knows us. He is familiar with all our ways. Psalm 139 clearly reminds us that God was not surprised, nor was He confused, when He made you. *You.*

God created us each to be unique and special. Those little quirks that you sometimes get teased about are really part of what makes you, *you*. Vonette Bright, in her little book called *The Woman Within*, said, "Every woman has a life imprint stamped on her hand by her Creator. Her imprint encompasses the details of her personality, her temperament, abilities, style, preferences and every other aspect of her life as a human being."[1]

The words of Psalm 139:3 remind us that God is familiar with *all* of our ways. Not only is God keenly aware of how messy or how organized you are, whether or not you have a speech impediment, or have fears of spiders or flying, He also knows your strengths. Your personality, what you are passionate about, what brings out creativity in you . . . God knows it all, because He created

Quirky, Wonderful You

Truth be known, we all have a lot of quirks, right? I recently shared this idea of having quirks with my Facebook friends and got some very funny responses. Here are just a few:

I've been called "grace" all my life because I can trip over air.

When I am thinking, pondering, concentrating, or am in the middle of a great book, I furrow my brow and everyone thinks I'm angry.

I shove used dryer sheets under my couch cushions. They still smell fresh when I get them out of the dryer with my clothes and I think they make the house smell good. My family and friends think I'm crazy when we use the pull out couch and there are a hundred dryer sheets to throw away.

When I get tired I twirl my hair with three fingers. I grab a piece of hair with my index finger and my thumb and rub the ends with my middle finger. If I am super tired you can find me with both hands twirling. It is always humorous because I never know that I am doing it (because I am tired) until someone informs me that I resemble Pippi Longstocking.

I sleep with a "blankie" that was made for me right after my daughter was put up for adoption. I've slept with it for twenty-four years.

Oh, Pat. I sleep with this stuffed mouse from when I was a kid. When I travel, my kids take over watching Mousey for me.

everything in you. Take a minute to soak in the truths contained within Psalm 139:3.

God has *purposes* for your unstuck gifts and talents.

God has *potential* for your unstuck quirks.

God has *plans that are good* for your unstuck weaknesses.

God *created* and *designed* unstuck you to be *you*.

Unstuck Truth #3: You are a one-of-a-kind unique design. You are enough.

Overflow Living in an Undertow World

You are a one-of-a-kind unique design. Live like you believe it, friend! The trouble is, as women we often find ourselves stuck in a personality and performance trap. We become more about what we do than who we are. We serve (overflow) so many people in so many ways that as much as we love and value them, we often lose ourselves (undertow) in the needs and demands of others. We become undone, unraveled, and unnoticed rather than taking the time to look deeper into who we are and what God has in mind for living life and moving from stuck to unstuck.

God is not only well aware of your ways, He created you with all of your ways for a reason. Let's take a look at our particular personalities using a little tool I use for my conferences called the Garden of Personality test. This tool will help as we move along to uncover those stuck places in your life and see how some of what we see as *stuck*, God sees as *potential*. This is your time; remember, it's all about you.

To take the Garden of Personality test, go across each line horizontally and check off the one attribute you believe *best* describes you. Then total each column vertically to see where you bloom. Remember, go with your initial "gut" reaction. That will give you a much more accurate response than overanalyzing it or choosing what you want to be like.

After tallying your checkmarks and realizing which column you had the greatest number of checkmarks for, what are you in God's garden? Are you a bumblebee, butterfly, ladybug, or hummingbird? Are you shocked at what you found in the test? Are you disappointed in what you discovered? Remember, if you could see what God sees, you would believe what God believes!

A Garden of Personality Test

☐ Likes control	☐ Enthusiastic	☑ Sensitive	☐ Constant
☐ Confident	☑ Visionary	☐ Calm	☑ Reserved
☐ Firm	☐ Energetic	☐ Nondemanding	☑ Practical
☑ Likes challenge	☐ Promoter	☑ Enjoys routine	☐ Factual
☑ Problem-solver	☐ Mixes easily	☑ Relational	☑ Perfectionistic
☐ Bold	☑ Fun-loving	☑ Adaptable	☑ Detailed
☐ Goal-driven	☐ Spontaneous	☑ Thoughtful	☑ Inquisitive
☐ Strong-willed	☑ Likes new ideas	☑ Patient	☑ Persistent
☑ Self-reliant	☐ Optimistic	☑ Good listener	☑ Sensitive
☐ Persistent	☐ Takes risks	☑ Loyal	☐ Accurate
☑ Takes charge	☑ Motivator	☐ Even-keeled	☐ Controlled
☐ Determined	☑ Very verbal	☑ Gives in	☐ Predictable
☐ Enterprising	☑ Friendly	☐ Indecisive	☐ Orderly
☐ Competitive	☐ Popular	☐ Dislikes change	☑ Conscientious
☑ Productive	☐ Enjoys variety	☑ Dry humor	☐ Discerning
☐ Purposeful	☑ Group-oriented	☑ Sympathetic	☐ Analytical
☐ Adventurous	☐ Initiator	☑ Nurturing	☐ Precise
☑ Independent	☐ Inspirational	☐ Tolerant	☐ Scheduled
☐ Action-oriented	☐ Likes change	☑ Peacemaker	☐ Deliberate

Total Score: _____ Total Score: _____ Total Score: _____ Total Score: _____

Now, find yourself in the garden!

Bumblebee	Butterfly	Ladybug	Hummingbird
Powerful Personality	People Personality	Peaceful Personality	Pondering Personality
Choleric	Sanguine	Phlegmatic	Melancholy

The Good News:	*The Good News:*	*The Good News:*	*The Good News:*
Problem Solver	Optimistic	Warm & Relational	Uncovers Excellence
Loves New Challenges	Energetic	Loyal	Able to Analyze and
Natural Leader	Motivator	Peace Lover	Clarify
Passionate	Future-oriented	Sensitive	Detailed and Focused
	Fun & Friendly	Attracted to the	Strategic Planner
The Tough Stuff:	Inspirational	Hurting	Dependable & Steady
Competitive		Great Listener	Organized
Can Be	*The Tough Stuff:*		
Confrontational	Can Be Manipulative	*The Tough Stuff:*	*The Tough Stuff:*
Too Busy	Needs Attention	Can Be Stuck in a Rut	Can Be Critical
Can Sting with Words	Impatient	Missed Opportunities	Glass Half Empty
	Avoids Details and	Too Many Details	High Expectations
	Follow-through	Indirect	Can Bog Down in the
		Communicator	Details

Imagine Me Set Free[R] | www.imaginemesetfree.com

Bumblebee. It is typically the "choleric," or as my mentor Florence Littauer calls it, the *powerful personality*, who thinks she can do everything better than what is being done.[2] Are you laughing because it is true in your life? Good! You are a natural problem solver—just like bees in your garden: always buzzing and busy at work. You love new challenges, are typically a natural leader, and are incredibly passionate. You typically want to instill the same potential and passion in others you see in yourself. This is a wonderful personality to have and most entrepreneurs have your exact personality . . . wow! Of course, there are some challenges to this personality type. If bumblebees are not careful they can sting, either intentionally or unintentionally.

Butterfly. "Girls Just Wanna Have Fun" . . . remember that song? Florence calls this the *people personality*. Also known as a "sanguine" personality, butterflies are incredibly optimistic, energetic, and make wonderful motivators. You typically are future-oriented, fun, and friendly. You inspire people and truly are a joy to be around, are very artistic, and never run short of ideas. Butterflies can have their trouble spots as well. Sometimes we butterflies flutter happily along our way, forgetting a few important details (like our child's school lunch) and follow-throughs (like turning off the car before getting out—I'm not saying I have ever *done* that, mind you!). For butterflies, things that don't smell so good and offer no fun are often ignored. Has that ever happened to you? Also, if butterflies are not careful, they can tend toward being manipulative and impatient and typically need a bunch of attention.

Ladybug. Ahhhh, relax . . . the peaceful ladybug, always a joy to find in the garden. They are also known as the *peaceful personality* or "phlegmatic," and are typically introspective and private. Ladybugs tend to be loyal, warm, relational, and sensitive. You tend to be a great listener, are drawn to those hurting around you, and crave peace. Ladybugs are usually steadfast and make faithful friends. But those tiny bugs can sometimes forget to fly to other areas in the garden. Have you ever been stuck in a rut and don't know how to get out? It's your personality, sister! You may have difficulty conversing because you are too cautious with your words, require too many details, and miss many opportunities because you can't see that you are surrounded by a big and beautiful garden and there is more than just the one plant you are happily skittering upon.

Hummingbird. This *perfect personality* is truly special in the Garden of Personality. They are treasured and appreciated as they beautifully pay attention to every detail. Hummingbirds flit precisely from this place to the next, always with purpose, always with an apparent plan in mind, just like you. Hummingbirds can also be known as "melancholy," and you are remarkable if you are one! You may have noticed you are very detail-oriented and focused on tasks at hand, and are very good at planning strategically. Others may have remarked about how dependable and steady you are, and your organizational skills have been praised on more than one occasion. Yet hummingbirds need to be mindful of their problem areas too. You may have a tendency to be overly critical of your own work or others', have extremely high expectations of yourself or others, and may be easily bogged down in the details of life. Hummingbirds tend to struggle with moodiness and depression and are inherently less social.

Are you ready? Do you like what you discovered, or do you wish you were more like another critter in God's Garden of Personality? You may not like the critter you are, but you are most definitely needed in God's kingdom, in His garden. For instance, you may want to be more of a butterfly because *everyone* loves them, especially at social gatherings, at parties, in school, and so forth, but if everyone were a fun-loving butterfly, no one would get anything done or know how to get anywhere, which is where hummingbirds come in so wonderfully. Or you may want to be a laid-back lady-bug, and be sensitive to a hurting world, but bumblebees are the ones who figure out what needs to be done to help them. Can you see how all the personality types are needed in order for tasks to be accomplished?

For instance, God birthed in me a desire to lead. I have been in some sort of leadership position all my life, starting with boss-ing my three younger sisters around. Soon after my surrender to Christ, I felt called to start Tampa's first pregnancy resource center, but I could have never done it alone. The ladybugs were needed in my life to ache with those who were hurting and be sensitive to their situation. The bumblebees were needed to come alongside me and figure out how to go about tackling the challenge of build-ing a center with fresh, new, and innovative ideas. Hummingbirds (my hubby is one of those!) were crucial for strategically planning how to get from the idea phase to the completion phase and pay-ing attention to details like legal filings and zoning requirements. And, yes, without butterflies to encourage me, and everyone else, along the way, we would have lost optimism and the motivation to continue. So, dear sister, you are *needed* in the kingdom and for a purpose, and that purpose is as unique as you are.

Remember what we decided in the last chapter about how we think? I want you to consciously choose to believe your ways are God's perfect way for you and part of your life for a specific rea-son—and that reason is *good*. Sure, you may have an overabundance of quirky behaviors, but delight in them. God certainly delights in them, just as He delights in you. As you carefully consider just how beautifully and artistically created you are, I want you to also think about your passions. God gave you those too, paired with your personality. And it is here at this joining of God-given passion and God-given personality where your destiny, your calling, can be discovered and embraced.

Sisters, you each were intricately made to make a difference in this world, and were created in the very way needed to make that God-given difference, that plan, that calling . . . your calling, your plan He has for *you*. Embrace your uniqueness. Celebrate your differences. Relish your quirks and wacky ways. Fully allow yourself to be you, for the world is dying to know hope and love . . . they are dying to be told by you, they are dying for you to be *you* and tell them about Him.

Be yourself . . . everyone else is taken. Solve problems; motivate and inspire; listen to the hurting; seek the reasons why. Be who God made you to be. Be God's beautiful, treasured, and cherished daughter.

Rejoice in the way you were made. Maybe take some time to journal a letter to God, thanking Him for each and every one of your quirky ways, every part of your unique personality, and every area you may not like. Thank Him for His wisdom and careful consideration when it came to making each and every part of you. As you begin to thank God, you will start to not only see what God sees in you but also begin to believe about yourself what God believes about you.

. . . .

Go to life-unstuck.com to share your Garden of Personality test results and to download the test to share with your family and friends.

4

UNSTUCK
Chick Chatter

Before a word is on my tongue you, LORD, know it completely.

Psalm 139:4

Words Contain Power

Whose pillow was this?

I had punched it and flipped it and rolled it around probably one hundred times and it still didn't fit my head. It was two a.m. and I was tossing and turning like the churning water in a Jacuzzi. But the truth is, it was my own bubbling brain keeping me awake. The internal chatter that kept me from sleep sounded like this: *Why did I say those words? Why did I speak like that to my dear friend? Why couldn't I just keep my mouth shut, Lord? Why? Why do I so often speak before I think, and will I ever* not *do that?*

I had been working on a ministry project with a dear friend, who just happened to also be my employee. We had deadlines and the pressure was building at a fast pace. Our gifts and talents were blending perfectly but time was moving faster than we were. The "telling" hour was fast approaching and people were going to see whether or not I, I mean *we*, were successful. They were going to judge my, I mean *our*, value to the team and I could not let that happen, could I? We had to get this task completed and it had to be *awesome* so that I, I mean *we*, would not disappoint anyone—and more importantly, we could shine and get lots of admiration and attention. Pressure was mounting along with my expectations of her, I mean *us*.

Then, of all the inconvenient things, she had a death in the family. Now what? I was to be stranded? I was going to have to finish this project alone? I was going to be totally responsible to the team without help? *I don't think so.*

A few "reasonable days" for grieving and mourning had passed. It was time to shake it off and get back to work. Right? Wrong. She just couldn't get a grip. She just couldn't get her mind back on the project. Finally, I figured enough was enough. I just needed to say something. As a friend, I needed to tell her what I thought about this whole mourning thing and to remind her of the ministry's policy of three days' time off for a death. I needed to tell her she had work to do. We had commitments and I, I mean *we*, had a reputation to protect.

I will never forget the look on her face or the tears that fell from her eyes as I declared the deadline on her grief and loss. I stated in no uncertain terms that she had a commitment to me and to this ministry. This ministry of healing, hope, and restoration had people to help and deadlines to meet and it was time to "get 'er done."

It seemed so logical to me, so clear—and something she really needed to hear to help her out of her pit. I was *helping* her.

My words, although it was not my intention, rammed into her heart like an arrow into a target and dug deep.

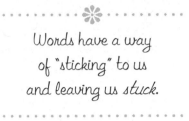

*Words have a way
of "sticking" to us
and leaving us stuck.*

Her face, her water-filled eyes, her shock at the character (or lack thereof) she saw unfold in me was what rolled around in my head on that uncomfortable pillow that night. *Why do I feel this way, Lord? I said the right thing, right? If so, why do I feel so ashamed? If not, how can I get those words back? How can I ever repair the damage that had just happened to our friendship?* Those words played over and over in my head and my heart, and time dragged by as sleep continued to elude me.

After the first few hours of my discussion with God about how I was right to say what I did, He began to stir my heart to repentance and the realization that my words had *not* been His words and my heart had *not* been His heart for my friend. Oh, no. *Ouch.* Honestly, it took a while.

I don't remember exactly how the repair took place in our friendship over the next few months. I am certain it was her grace and forgiveness, not mine, that won the day, but this I do remember: God's quiet, loving Spirit started stirring that night to work the weight of my words out in my heart and life over the next few years.

It wasn't very long after that occurrence when she and I were once again planted in some big ministry undertaking and my turn came to lose a loved one. The loss hit me like a truck. I couldn't breathe for weeks. I cried day and night for many months afterward. I remember walking up to my friend at the funeral, our friendship long since recovered, grabbing hold of her, and crying, "I am so sorry, I am so sorry. I had no idea."

Words have power and God knows it. He knows that He created us with a voice, a mouth, and a tongue, and all the physical mechanics it takes to unleash either life or death.

God Knows the Way of Our Say

God knows everything surrounding our every word before it is spoken. As Charles Spurgeon put it, "The unformed word, which lies within the tongue like a seed in the soil, is certainly and completely known to the Great Searcher of hearts."[1]

Wow. This means God is well aware of not only what is actually going to be said but the *intention* behind the words. He knows why I responded "Fine" to my husband when I was nowhere near "fine." He knows when I am hypocritical in my speech instead of genuine, when I am passive-aggressively responding instead of graceful, when I hurt someone deeply and intentionally with my words just to be revengeful. Why is any of this important? Because, sister, as you may have already discovered, words have power.

Whoever coined the phrase "talk is cheap" was a liar. The words we say are incredibly powerful and amazing tools. Talking can change lives and even change the world! Think about some amazing ways words have changed lives:

When JFK asked us what we could do for our country? An entire nation was rallied.

When MLK wrote his letter from Birmingham, Alabama? Different races were challenged to treat everyone with equality.

When Neil Armstrong took his first steps (and spoke his first words) on the moon? The world took notice of what humans could achieve.

When Jesus said, "It is finished" on a hilltop? An entire human race was forgiven.

"It's Just My Opinion"

I think you get the idea. Words are not cheap; in fact, they are quite *expensive*. Whether words cost something to the speaker, the spoken about, or the spoken to, there is always a price tag. Words can inspire you to do great things, so they cost you time and money. Words can convict you to stop certain actions, so they cost you time and your patience. Words can heal broken relationships and can set you free, so they cost you your past wounds and patterns.

However, not all words we have experienced have been so uplifting. You already know about those words. You have felt them, right? We have all felt the sting of words that pierce right to the core of our being and take the breath right out of us. They may have been subtle or may have been rather direct, but you know the potency of words: the immeasurable and unmistakable ability words have to hurt, to wound, to crush. I am sure you can recall moments when you felt the brutal sting of words flung at you like it was yesterday.

Words can leave us stuck or unstuck.

We have all been on the other side of words that leave us stuck in shame, stuck in fear—stuck in hopelessness. God's Word warns us about words that leave us and others stuck:

> The tongue also is a fire, a world of evil among the parts of the body. It corrupts the whole body, sets the whole course of one's life on fire, and is itself set on fire by hell. (James 3:6)

Ouch. We have probably all experienced the phrase from our mothers or teachers at some point in our lives (or even spoken it ourselves): "Watch your mouth, young lady!" Do you remember ever thinking,

How in the world can I watch my mouth? It is on my face! Sometimes words just fly out so fast there is no way I could ever "watch" them.

I recall a speaking engagement where I was standing on the stage in front of hundreds of women, passionately proclaiming my speech, when I heard myself say, "She was out of that place so fast she was like a you-know-what out of hell!"

Umm . . . what did I just say? Oh my gosh! I meant a bat *out of* you-know-where!

I was mortified at my slip of the tongue but later cracked up in the privacy of my room. Good ole Pat, she would *never* say the "bat" word on stage. She's a "good girl," a "Christian," a "Bible teacher."

God knows the intent behind our words before they are spoken; He also knows how the intent was placed there to begin with. The Bible says "what the mouth speaks, the heart is full of" (Luke 6:45). When we fill our hearts with good stuff, good stuff comes out. The truth is I live *stuck* or *unstuck* depending upon what is in my heart.

Uncover the Power of Words and Unpack the Potential of Praise!

The Bible says that our words of praise and thanksgiving honor God and are directly connected to our life unstuck. Remember when we talked in chapter 2 about how our heart leads to our thoughts? Here we are looking at how our thoughts lead to our words. I am constantly learning to *think* before I speak—both internally and externally, where I know that what is in my heart is going to come out. Another way to say that is this:

> But the things that come out of a person's mouth come from the heart, and these defile them. (Matt. 15:18)

What is in our *heart* will be what we *think*, and what we *think* is eventually what we will *say*. I think I've said it before but I need

58

to say it once more (I know that rhymes): life unstuck starts in the heart, leads to a thought, and eventually ends up in the mouth.

We must think as God thinks. We must also say what God says! We are uniquely and especially made for a specific purpose. Don't forget the truths that we are building upon here—or rather, that are growing from our roots.

Unstuck Truth #4: You can change what you believe about yourself when you change what you say about yourself.

Here is an example of how this works. There are women who have struggled with their weight for years who begin to identify themselves, to think of themselves, as *fat*. Being *fat* is how they see themselves inside and out. If our internal dialog doesn't change, our external dialog will not change either. Even after losing weight, some women continue to think of themselves and see themselves as fat, ugly, or unlovable, and still *say with their mouths* that they are fat, and they never seem to lose enough weight because *fat* is how they have defined themselves for so long. They label themselves this way because it was what they said about themselves, over and over and over. Those records we replay endlessly in our minds identify who we believe we are.

Dear sister, there is hope for you, and for me. I don't know about you, but there was a time when I believed I was beyond hope, that I would never be truly loved just as I am, and that I could never escape the guilt and shame of my past—but I was *so* wrong, and so glad I was! As I have allowed the Word of God to transform me, from my heart (intentions) and flowing outward through my mouth, verses like this one have become my daily prayer:

> Set a guard over my mouth, Lord;
> keep watch over the door of my lips. (Ps. 141:3)

And then some of these verses became my challenges as I pursued God and being unstuck just as He was pursuing me. God instructs us in Ephesians not to let *any* unwholesome talk come out of our mouth and to speak *only* what builds others up. That's a huge unstuck challenge!

Letting these truths bury themselves in my heart, spurred on by my personal study of Psalm 139, caused me to truly be more aware of every word that comes out of my mouth, and I am encouraging you with the same. I began by consciously saying truth about myself as I was reading what God said about me. I no longer said I was never going to be loved just the way I was. Instead, I chose to say, "I am fully loved and accepted just the way I am. Not only that, but I was made this way for God's good pleasure and for His purpose!" Talk about a shift! Now, it didn't happen overnight, but it did happen and is *continuing* to happen. God is always working on me. This is another thing I found to be true:

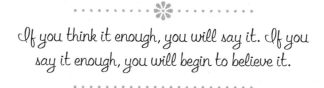

If you think it enough, you will say it. If you say it enough, you will begin to believe it.

So let us say the truth, and say it *a lot*. You didn't get stuck overnight but change can begin immediately. What you say about yourself not only reflects what you believe but also directs your life, or can *re*direct your life.

So begin right now, today, and you can begin to redirect your life simply by speaking the truth over your life. We have opportunities every single day to help someone else get *unstuck* with our words.

Say something worth saying, something encouraging, uplifting, and praiseworthy.

Remember, this verse from David's heart reminds us that God knows the *way* of our say. Change the direction of your day with what you say, for yourself, your family, your coworkers, and your child's school—every place you go. Your words have power, so use His power to say something worthy, something eternal, something that will lead others to Him.

And that, dear sister, is life unstuck!

. . . .

Visit life-unstuck.com to request a list of stuck vs. unstuck words.

5

UNSTUCK

Security

You hem me in behind and before, and you lay your hand upon me.

Psalm 139:5

My husband and I recently joined our middle son and his family of five, plus two canine critters, for a day of hiking in the park. Andy and his lovely wife, Bethany, met us at the front gate with our three "G babies" tagging along behind at decreasing stepladder heights, like baby ducks trailing their mamma. Their two dogs made up the tail of the family line with eyes wide open, excitedly looking for unsuspecting squirrels. One of Andy's dogs, Sadie, being a bit of an old lady, is always faithful to stick close to the group while the other, a puppy named Oreo, has the energy of, well, a puppy, and was not quite as reliable, so Andy had her captured by a short leash.

We started our hike through the beautiful and nicely marked paths that made it easy to know where we should be and where we shouldn't be. Our G babies, as we call them, ranged at the time from ages seven to three. Seven-year-old Mikala and four-year-old Kai were much like faithful dog Sadie, content to stay with the group, enjoying the flora and fauna and a few good outdoor friends within the clearly marked boundaries of the Florida Parks Authority. On the other hand, three-year-old Bella was much more like Oreo and refused to be contained by a silly old *path*. Bella was stopping to pick up a roly-poly one minute and the next running ahead to chase a hopeless duck or lizard. Andy eventually got so tired of chasing after Bella to keep her safely on the path that he took the leash off Oreo and put it on her! It was adorable, and Bella giggled at her daddy's act of genius.

As we read David's words I can't help but picture our Abba Father as David might have been picturing Him on the day he wrote this verse. Studies tell us he was possibly trapped in a dark cave, hiding from his enemies.

You hem me in behind and before, and you lay your hand upon me. (Ps. 139:5)

Most of the time when we use the phrase "hemmed in," it doesn't have such a warm and fuzzy connotation. Many times people use it to describe their frustrations at work or school, unusually heavy traffic on a commute, or in general when referring to stress. Because of our cultural context, when we read these words of how God hems us in we may miss out on their blessing. You see, David was not only a man after God's own heart and a soon-to-be king, he was also a warrior. He understood what it meant to be in the heat of battle and needing protection. Lastly, David was also a daddy, just like my son, and knew how much he wanted to protect his own kids from danger or evil. So I want you to take a moment and try to read this verse from a father's perspective, and a tender, loving father at that.

You hem me in! You place your hand of blessing on my head!

Our Father God has made a provision for his daughters to never fear any external circumstance because they are fully surrounded by His protection. He has created a path, if you will, that envelops each one of us in the safety of His love. Not only that, but this Father places His hand on His beloved daughter in order to give a reassuring touch whenever it is needed and to let the whole world know this child belongs to Him.

Let's make this personal, OK?

God surrounds you with His presence, His protection, His love, and His acceptance because He loves you. Your heavenly Father can never stop this loving affection He has for you because it is part of who He is. God is love, and His love never fails and never gives up on you, or on me. So this idea of being "hemmed in" is for our good, done out of the abundant love of our Abba Father. Not only do we benefit from His protection, His provision, and His love but when He puts His hand upon us we are immediately unstuck from all that keeps us from enjoying the benefits of His protection and love.

Being "hemmed in" by God keeps us reassured and quieted, and we can once again be emboldened to face our next steps of the journey.

Unstuck in God's Grip

God's grip lets the entire world know you belong to Him . . . and there is nothing that can change that. His hand declares to everyone who has eyes to see and ears to hear that you have God's heart, His attention, and His blessings.

We have considered how intimately God knows us, how He knows our thoughts before we do, how He knows all of our quirks—and He knows all of this because He made us, He made you, just the way you are. And just like any good daddy, God loves to bless His kids. He loves to direct your gaze toward your favorite bird flying by, just because it makes you smile. He loves to make your favorite flowers bloom because He loves to see you enjoy their scent. He loves to answer your prayers because He loves to see you jump for joy. God loves you so dearly and so deeply, and He loves you just the way you are. However, because so many of us don't believe we are lovable, we don't believe we are loved.

David is articulating just how loved by God he feels. One version of the Bible says it this way:

> You go before me and follow me.
> You place your hand of blessing on my head.
> (Ps. 139:5 NLT)

Unstuck Truth #5: God has been, is, and always will be present. He will never let you go.

We are clearly seeing a very important truth about life unstuck as David declares that God has him *hemmed in*. David is being completely honest and transparent with his heart and his life and his words. He has openly exposed himself to God's love. David understands that a very real God knows a very real David. A very real God knows a very real you, my sister. He has you "hemmed in" if—and this is a big if—you have surrendered your life to Him.

Our unstuck life in Christ depends upon our unstuck surrender. This was news to me; maybe it is to you too.

Unstuck through Surrender

I grew up in Savannah, Georgia, home of dripping moss, hot pink azaleas, and awesome seafood. God chose a world of women for me right from the beginning. I had a dad hidden in the house somewhere, but he never held a majority vote in the hormonal jungle of our home. Childhood was pretty uneventful for me in a lower-end, middle-class world of upper-end, high-class friends. I always seemed to be reaching for something I couldn't grasp. I was very ambitious and had big dreams from the time I was little that mostly had to do with being my own boss as quickly as possible. For as long as I can remember, I was looking for something but couldn't seem to figure out what it was. Although we considered ourselves a Christian family, our church attendance was sporadic at best. We went to vacation Bible school and celebrated the holidays, but for me it was very shallow. I had little to no understanding of what God had to do with my personal life, if anything. I certainly never considered myself "in His grip," or anyone else's for that matter.

I reached into the life of an "adult" at the young age of fifteen and became the teenage wife of my high school sweetheart at sixteen. He came from a very broken family background and had much influence on the choices I made. Although most of the things that came out of that relationship were not so good, the one good thing we created together was an adorable little boy who quickly became the light of my life. My young husband, however, did not want to remain a husband for long and took off for the opposite coast before our son made the transition from bottle to cup. My little boy and I were left to the rescue of my parents who, having had only girls, were quick to embrace a little boy into the family. He was, in fact, the sun, moon, and stars to them. They joyfully helped me take care of my son, complete my high school education, and attend our local college. It was there that I met my future husband. Our relationship was passionately propelled from the beginning, and having no moral boundaries set us up for some very bad choices and behaviors. We fell in love but I was still *stuck* on being "in charge" of my own life. I finally hit what I thought would be the bottom of a pit when I chose to have an abortion to cover our immoral lifestyle. I'll tell you more about that later, but for now let me say that the choices I made while trying to run my own path freely, like little Bella in the park that day, literally resulted in death.

What I didn't understand during those years of my life is that God does "hem us in" but we must choose to stay in His grip. He gives us free will. He will allow our stubborn, disobedient hearts to take as much "leash" as we demand. It's our choice to nestle into His grip and stay within His protective embrace.

Little did I know at the time that the enemy of life was quite happy with my random running and capable of taking me even deeper into the dark, bottomless pit I was in. From age twenty-three to thirty, I gave him party time in my life, until one dark and shame-filled night my Savior, who not only knew His way around that dark part of my life but was also not afraid to go there, called my name loud and clear.

I recognized His voice from my childhood days of Sunday school, vacation Bible school, and church on Easter Sunday and Christmas Eve. His sweet embrace overwhelmed my darkness, my broken life, and my heart. I crumbled into His protection that very night and never looked back.

My actual born again experience happened at a church women's retreat after a beautiful woman saw my stuck self hiding out in the Sunday school wing with my two sons, petrified to enter the "big church," and invited me to join her at the event. After hearing the clear truth of the gospel and for the first time understanding my need to respond to what Christ had done for me, I went running— barreling, actually—to the altar. I surrendered my heart to Christ that day and have been caught up in the power of His love ever since.

I chose to be in His grip. I chose to be "hemmed in." I chose to surrender all to Jesus. I still choose, now, to be in His grip, to be hemmed in, and to surrender all as well.

Have *you* made that choice, my sister? Have you ever made that personal, intentional choice to surrender your life to Christ?

If not—today is your day!

•••••

This walk of our salvation is an amazing journey, a kaleidoscope of change and transformation that is beyond description and ever unfolding. Life unstuck requires that you understand there was always a plan—a Rescuer—and His name is Jesus. He has fulfilled every one of God's promises of what the Rescuer would be like, look like, act like, come from, you name it! Jesus spent years telling people how much God loved them, how God never stopped loving them, and how He ached for His children to once more trust His heart toward them.

What a message of hope!

When you encounter the life-changing, all-encompassing, never-ending, never-fading love the Father has for you, His daughter—life gets unstuck. Not only does God's love rescue you, but it finally completes you and it gets you unstuck.

God's love for us has never changed, wavered, waned, or even grown deeper. God's love is and always has been perfect and full, steadfast and true. We don't really "deserve" God's love. We can never be good enough for such a righteous and amazing God. His love is a *gift*. God loved me in the middle of my immorality and sin. He still loves me in my sin. He loves you in the middle of yours. However, when we receive forgiveness, it is then our hearts are softened, our eyes are truly opened, and we can finally perceive God's love, blessings, and delight in us—and receive them. We are then free to pursue God, to know God, to have an intimate relationship with Him, and to be utterly set free.

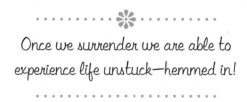

Once we surrender we are able to experience life unstuck—hemmed in!

Choose Life Unstuck by Fully Surrendering to His Loving Grip

If you have never surrendered your life completely to Jesus, no matter what I share in the pages of this book you will never be completely unstuck. He is your Creator, your Savior, your Friend, and your only hope!

To give Him your life today, take these steps right now and please, oh my dear sister, *please* contact me at life-unstuck.com and let me know that you have. I have a free gift to send, from me to you!

Steps to the Cross

1. God created you and loves you. (Gen. 1:26–27; John 3:16–18)
2. We've fallen from our original glory. (Gen. 3:1,13; Rom. 3:23)
3. Jesus came to rescue you from darkness and captivity. (Col. 1:12–14)
4. Jesus is your only hope for abundant and eternal life. (John 14:6)
5. You must choose life. (John 1:12–13; 5:24)

When God hems us in, all around, He does it to give us boundaries so we will have greater peace of mind, a greater sense of security, and greater freedom to play and just be His kids. It is within God's protective borders that we have the freedom to let go, to play, to run freely, and to truly enjoy our lives to the fullest without the slightest hint of fear. So let go. Embrace that indescribable love and acceptance God holds out to you. Run to your Rescuer. Believe you are loved. Be a child . . . and let your heavenly Father show the world you belong to Him.

Please don't forget! If God has used this book to secure your salvation, I would love to know! Visit life-unstuck.com.

6

UNSTUCK
Wonder

Such knowledge is too wonderful for me, too lofty for me to attain.

Psalm 139:6

Prepare to be Amazed

I recently had one of my "G girls," my granddaughter Mikala, spend the night. I was busy in my kitchen preparing dinner for her when I heard Mikala call out to me from the upstairs guest room.

"G! Prepare to be amazed!"

Be still my beating heart! Just those words alone caused my body to tingle with anticipation and glee. I knew something was up, since "not a creature had been stirring, not even a mouse" for the past half hour. Something told me this was going to be good, so I grabbed and readied my phone's camera. An Instagram moment was about to be born. Sure enough, as I rounded the corner from the kitchen to the steps, there she was. She slowly descended the staircase with her little chin pointed toward the ceiling just to add that extra air of superiority, and her long brown locks bounced behind her. She embraced her very best beauty queen pose with her arm lingering halfway between sky and earth, and her oversized high heels pointed in the direction of her audience. She was slowly but intentionally making her dramatic stroll down the staircase, dressed from tip to toe with every kind of sparkly and twinkly dress-up garb she had been able to dig up.

I have always kept a play box of dress-up clothes for my "Gs" to tear into that had been handed down from my daughter, Julianna. I have relished every moment of seeing those gowns and garments draped upon my beloved babies for over twenty-five years. On this special day, in that special moment, Mikala had discovered them all and she was determined to savor every morsel of dramatic delivery her tiny little five-year-old mind and body could design.

I was breathless. She was the most adorable ballerina. Or was it cheerleader? I think a mix of the two worked beautifully. I was most definitely amazed! Not to mention enthralled, in love, and giddy with joy that she was *mine*. She is my G girl and my treasured possession.

Do you feel treasured like my Mikala? If you are like most women I have encountered in my ministry over the past twenty-plus years, probably not. You, instead, probably feel *un-treasured* and *un-enthralling* to those around you because of mean words or actions you have experienced over your tough years. However, I am here to give you hope.

The way I felt over Mikala—enthralled, in love, giddy—that, my sister, is how God feels about you, and I can prove it. Right now! Your heavenly Father is looking upon you and He is seeing something spectacular. He is seeing a daughter who has captured His heart and stolen His breath away. He is looking upon a treasured possession and the love of His life. And you can bet your bottom dollar He is always ready with His camera too. Instagram sensation, here *you* go.

As I have sunk my head, heart, and heels into the study of Psalm 139, I have been reminded of Habakkuk 1:5, where in response to a complaint issued by the prophet Habakkuk, God says:

> Look at the nations and watch—
> and be *utterly* amazed.
> For I am about to do something in your days
> that you would not believe,
> even if you were told. (emphasis added)

You see, just as God is captured by us, He also longs to capture our attention. He delights in surprising us with His goodness, His sovereignty, and His power. Think about it. Have you ever witnessed a hurricane? How about a tornado or a shooting star? Have you ever watched a baby being born or marveled at a seahorse? How about a field of summer flowers on the side of a mountain? We all have experienced, at some point or another, overwhelming awe at God's creation. The wonderful thing about being in awe of God's creation is how God longs to stir up that kind of response in us. He does not do these wonderful things, nor do "the heavens declare the glory of God; the skies proclaim the work of His hands" (Ps. 19:1) merely for our enjoyment. No, He lovingly reveals them to us so we, in return, would further seek His heart and know His heart's passion is . . . us. You!

Unstuck Truth #6: God delights in amazing you with His love.

Have you ever read how God responded to the ongoing dialogue between Job and his three "friends"? I love those verses that follow my Bible's headline, "The Lord Speaks," in Job 38 and following. For a dose of amazement, take a minute to read them. God loves to captivate us with His handiwork and awaken us to His fiery fanfare.

As we point our toes toward the glory of God's greatness revealed in Psalm 139, I want to inspire you to prepare your heart for some unstuck wonder. I want to call out to you from the staircase of these pages and challenge you to "prepare to be amazed." Get the camera of your heart and mind ready to capture the moment and seize the drama of David's words as he shares his snapshot from history with us. God wants, once again, to show you His glory, His goodness, His personal investment in *you*. He wants to leave you breathless, enthralled, in love, and giddy with joy to be His daughter, His treasured possession.

The first part of verse 6 says, "Such knowledge is too wonderful for me." What knowledge is David talking about? The past five verses, of course. The knowledge of how David is fully known; how his thoughts are discerned before they even register in his brain; what is truly in David's heart, his intentions, his words, how he is protected by God . . . everything! How does God do it? David doesn't quite know, but he *does* know such godly knowledge is too wonderful for him. He is awed by God's knowledge of him, not to mention how God knew (and knows) everyone else with the same depth. Our God truly is *awesome*. That is the point David is making here. But do not stop here, sister. There is much more to this wonderful knowledge. This knowledge is not like what most of us have experienced when our families, friends, spouses, and sisters know us and all our ugly secrets, shortcomings, and failures. That type of knowledge sometimes leads to some sort of judgment, withdrawal, or shunning—whether temporary or permanent. But your heavenly Father is completely different. He knows it all and still delights in you and loves you, and you are the apple of His eye.

Let this Scripture cause your heart to be *amazed*.

> The Lord your God is with you,
> the Mighty Warrior who saves.

> He will take great delight in you;
> in his love he will no longer rebuke you,
> but will rejoice over you with singing. (Zeph. 3:17)

Psalm 149 says God *delights* in you. Luke 12 says He is *pleased* with you. Psalm 17 says you are the *apple of His eye.* Jeremiah 31:3 says God loves you with an *everlasting* love.

Are those words not amazing, encouraging, and mind-blowing all at the same time? They may be a bit hard to believe at first, but they are true, and the truth *will* get you unstuck, just like Jesus said it would.

As women, we usually focus on the outside before the inside— and it's not what you may initially think. Women deal with much in life and we are, at times, consumed by what the *outside world* thinks of us—and just for a change, let's not bring our physical bodies into this. We want to make sure our performance is acceptable at work. We worry about what the Bible study will think of us if we don't show up. What will our child's teacher say if we cannot be a chaperone? What about our husband, if we forget to have the suit pressed before his presentation or we forgot to pay that bill? What about our friends when we do or do not choose to watch a certain television show? You see, the "outside" sometimes consumes us and we worry about changing those things, but no real change actually occurs. Again, God is different. He says the only way to change is from the *inside* out. This transformation happens when we believe what God says about us: He loves us, accepts us, and delights in us. God is very interested in what you think about, especially what you think about His thoughts toward you.

Unstuck Love

Ever since we were little girls, we have been bombarded by the idea of real love, usually wrapped up in a perfect setting of princesses and princes, evil villains, and true love always winning in the end. Remember Cinderella, Snow White, Little Orphan Annie? They romance us as little ones, and then we grow up a bit and find ourselves seeking to fill the longing for true love in other places, unfulfilling places, as the reality of life and real men sinks in and we stop dreaming. We believe such a wonderful love story is impossible, fatherly acceptance doesn't exist, and nothing good is possible for us. Marriage is difficult, *very* difficult. Being told you are loved by a distant father or mother is the aching of your heart. Happy endings end with the slam of a door, the signing of a document, and broken hearts and homes around us. And yet we are still drawn to stories of love, where the beloved is pursued relentlessly and love wins. Am I right?

Have you noticed, either in your own life or watching a dear friend or family member, how people change when they know they are loved? You can watch another woman blossom right before your eyes as she realizes she is loved, accepted, and desired by her beloved. Love is the safety net that allows us to be spontaneous, to take chances, to attempt great feats, to reveal our true selves, to become more than we ever thought possible. If this can happen with human love, which is imperfect, imagine what could transpire in your life, in your world, in your heart when you realize God loves you, accepts you, and desires you. Watch out, world! You are about to be revealed, in all your loved glory and beauty. Soak up these words, dear girl:

> Who shall separate us from the love of Christ? Shall trouble or hardship or persecution or famine or nakedness or danger or sword? As it is written: "For your sake we face death all day long; we are considered as sheep to be slaughtered." No, in all these things we are more than conquerors through him who loved us. For I am convinced that neither death nor life, neither angels nor demons, neither the present nor the future, nor any powers, neither height nor depth, nor anything else in all creation, will

be able to separate us from the love of God that is in Christ Jesus our Lord. (Rom. 8:35–39)

My prayer for you, and for myself, is that you would allow these truths to sink deeply into your heart, into your spirit, and *transform* you. Choose one verse at a time and meditate upon it. Ponder each and every word and truly digest how each word applies to you. For instance, take Psalm 103:8 (ESV). Applying each word to you might look like this:

The Lord (my Lord, my Master, my King)

is merciful (is full of compassion, forbearance, kindness, forgiveness)

and gracious, (shows kindness and courtesy, is friendly and favorable toward me)

slow to anger (takes a long time or lacks speed in becoming displeased or belligerent, wrathful, resentful, or exasperated with me)

and abounding in (is filled with, has in great quantities, is rich and well supplied)

steadfast (fixed in direction, firmly established, unwavering)

love (profoundly tender, passionately affectionate, deeply attached; passionate for; adoring).

And all of this is specifically toward *you*. God is merciful toward *you*. God is gracious toward *you*. God is slow to anger toward *you*. God is abounding in immovable love toward *you*, his precious and treasured daughter. Now can you begin to identify with David when he said such knowledge is too wonderful for him? That it is too lofty to attain, because it is almost too good to be true, but *is true*? This is the knowledge that transforms us, changes us, and makes us new, from the inside out. What would happen to your walk; to your life; to how you relate to your family, your coworkers, your friends, and your church if you walked confidently in your identity as a beloved one of God? What if you traipsed down the stairs and confidently proclaimed, "Be prepared to be amazed!" in all your sparkly glory? The answer is simple: you would change the world.

David knew he was loved and led Israel to love the one true God. David changed the world.

Moses knew he was loved and led a captive people out of Egypt and to the edge of the Promised Land. Moses changed the world.

Nehemiah knew he was loved and rallied Israel to rebuild the city wall in a little over two months. Nehemiah changed the world.

Deborah knew she was loved and judged Israel well, and led them to victory. Deborah changed the world.

Mary Magdalene knew she was loved and poured her dowry over Jesus's feet. Mary Magdalene changed the world.

The Samaritan woman encountered true love in Christ and led her entire town to the Savior. The Samaritan woman changed the world.

Paul encountered the love of Christ and took the gospel to the Gentiles. Paul changed the world.

Jesus's disciples knew they were loved and took His message to the rest of the world. The disciples changed the world.

This begs the question: What can God do through you when you are unstuck and captured by His love for you? When you become like my little Mikala, relishing the adoration of her grandma, knowing just being her little Mikala-self brings me joy?

You can change the world!

Nothing is impossible for God, including healing your wounded heart and changing it from a heart of stone, protected from secrets and wounds and harsh words, to a heart of flesh, actively receiving and giving away God's love to others.

So, be amazed at unstuck love—God's love. Let God love you. Let God's love transform you. Parade yourself, dressed to the nines, in the presence of your heavenly Father, knowing just being yourself brings Him great joy and delight, and then let Him dance with you as He sings over you. Change the world, my friend!

Section Two

Peace with the Past

Psalm 139:7–12

Where can I go from your Spirit?
   Where can I flee from your presence?
If I go up to the heavens, you are there;
   if I make my bed in the depths, you are there.
If I rise on the wings of the dawn,
   if I settle on the far side of the sea,
even there your hand will guide me,
   your right hand will hold me fast.
If I say, "Surely the darkness will hide me
   and the light become night around me,"
even the darkness will not be dark to you;
   the night will shine like the day,
   for darkness is as light to you.

7

UNSTUCK
Peace

Where can I go from your Spirit? Where can I flee from your presence?

Psalm 139:7

My heart was pounding and my hands were completely numb from their tight grip on the car door armrest. Nonetheless, my "awesome mom" meter was off the charts. My sixteen-year-old son, Tim, glowed with pride behind the wheel of my brand-new sports car.

We were hitting the road for a long trip from Tampa to Chicago, and he was beyond excited. Me? I was beyond terrified. Tim was a good driver but a bit on the reckless side, like the time he took his buddies "butt skiing" behind his Jeep on the new golf course behind our home. This trip, though, he drove beautifully all the way to Illinois. As we approached Chicago, we noticed the sun's rapid descent behind those beautiful buildings, creating Chicago's exciting, stunning skyline. Being the official map reader (before the days of Google Maps and GPS), I could see we had veered off course as Tim merged into the fast-moving Chicago traffic.

"Honey, I need to take it from here," I reasonably declared as Mom. "It is getting dark and we are lost."

"Mom, no! I can do this," was his unreasonable son response. "Just tell me where to turn."

Much to my dismay, I surrendered to his response. He continued to drive and I continued to clutch the armrest all the tighter with each passing mile. Darker and darker the sky became, and "lost-er" and "lost-er" we turned out to be. Finally, amidst the very dark and tangled interstates surrounding the Windy City, I lost all "reasonable mom" behavior and yelled, "Pull over right now! I have to drive."

My teenager obeyed and exited stage right. We drove off the interstate onto an exit ramp no one else seemed to want. It was dark as molasses with no lights in sight. We were *so* lost. Then, out of nowhere, lights! Very bright and huge lights! It was all we could see and they were coming straight toward us. It took us practically no time at all to realize the source of those lights coming at us head-on . . . an airplane!

Somehow, my teenage son and I found ourselves facing down a runway of O'Hare International Airport, without a place to turn around, and we were smack dab in the path of an airplane making its journey into the sky.

Oh my.

"Turn around, Tim, turn around," I screamed with all the finesse of a freaked-out mamma.

It's so funny when I hear those words today on my car's GPS: "Rerouting, Rerouting!" It always reminds me of this day. Tim screeched on the brakes and, like a racecar driver, flipped that little sports car 180 degrees. I don't want to know where he got *that* skill.

Tim headed back toward the interstate without even looking back to see if an airplane was approaching our tailpipe. Could this get any worse? He pulled the car off on the side of the road, and it was then we became more aware of our surroundings. We were actually on a service road, which had a very high fence separating vehicles from the airplanes. That fence was keeping us from going down the wrong path, even though we didn't immediately see it. That night I was left with a life truth that would change my life forever.

A Human Experience of a Divine Presence

Take a minute if you will and go back to the beginning of this section and really read the words from Psalm 139:7–12. They are about to take us on a life-changing trip *backward*.

David, during some of his darkest hours and most frightening moments, reveals his true understanding of "The God Who Sees." To start, David asks a rhetorical question about fleeing from God's Spirit and His presence. Why? Why does David even consider the possibility of getting away from God's presence? What could be so bad, so shameful, so embarrassing to David as to make him want to flee from God?

I can relate to David; can you? As I have learned more about the man behind the giant-slaying clothes, it almost seems as though he is looking for opportunities or places to hide. As he runs through this mental checklist, he comes to the realization: there is no place to hide from God, and nothing escapes God's watchful gaze. Nothing I do or have done escapes God's gaze, either. There have been so many times I have looked back and realized God saw me *there*, and then I tremble. I have been in some pretty bad places and made some pretty bad choices. Maybe you haven't made so many bad choices but bad choices were made for you or upon you. Or maybe these words resonate with you today. Maybe there are some stuck places going on in your life right now that cause you to want to hide from God. Like that time you lost your temper, the time you thought no one was watching, the lie that spiraled out of control.

What we learn of David in this passage is that he definitely had his moments of thinking it best to hide from God. David was a brave warrior; he worshiped God with his whole being; he is in the lineage of Christ . . . yet we know that in a moment of shame and fear, he murdered the captain of his guard. In a moment of uncontrolled lust, he committed adultery.

God knew everything David did—the good, bad, and ugly. Just like He knows everything you have done—the good, bad, and ugly.

Those bad choices, whether made by us or on us, often leave us *stuck* in some past event that, unless dealt with, holds us back from all God has for us. God wants to use our past to overcome the enemy, and I can prove it.

God wants your past unstuck and available to be used under His anointing and for your destiny. God desires to use our past, not to shame or condemn us but to break the stronghold the enemy has on our testimony and use our story for His glory.

If Tim and I had not turned around to see where we had come from, we would have never arrived at where we were going. If we are not willing to look back and let God rewrite our memories, we will never fully arrive at our divine destiny and never see what God *can* do with our heartbreaks and mistakes.

As I settled this truth into my heart, I understood how the light "came on" for David. Within these beautifully penned words, I realized that *when we see ourselves as God sees us, we will believe about ourselves what God believes about us.* When we truly comprehend that when He looks at us He sees a woman He loves, we no longer have the desire to hide from Him. Wow! Just like David, we have to allow that truth to nestle into our hearts and settle down, to take root.

We have to make a choice to trust God with our past—our deepest secrets, greatest losses, and worst choices.

That is when healing happens.

However, many of us don't want to go there. Many times I didn't want to reveal my hurt or let God heal me because it hurt too badly . . . the wounds were too dark, and revisiting those dark times was too painful. Yes, it is difficult, and even the Bible clearly states such a process is work, but work worth the journey.

●●●●●

Over the many years I have served in women's ministry, I have discovered a startling trend. When it comes to running and hiding from the past, sometimes those of us in the church are just as bad, if not worse, than those outside the church. Of course we declare that Jesus has saved us and forgiven us, including forgiving our past. The problem is, many times we stop there and neglect to allow Him to heal our past and use it for our present and future. Revelation 12:11 says, in essence, that if we can't share our testimony we will live a life that is stuck in the past. If "the word of your testimony" is stuck, you can't share as God calls you to share. You are *stuck*.

In Genesis 16, the Bible tells Hagar's story. Hagar was a woman much like me, and maybe like you, who knew what it was like to run from the past. In this story we discover how her dreams for family, youth, and love did not go the way she planned—the way she had dreamed since she was a girl.

We see in Hagar's story how she responded to a seemingly hopeless situation by running away as hard and fast as she could. I don't think she stopped to consider where she might end up or what consequences her choice would bring. She simply responded to her pain and loss with desperation and panic. I can identify with her because I have been like Hagar. Perhaps you have too. Have you responded to some memory, loss, or heartache the way Hagar did—by running? Did you hide those heartbreaks away, never to see the light of day? Perhaps you always feared that, should they ever be uncovered, you and those you are trying to protect would simply fall apart. Just like Hagar, many of us have felt lost, alone, and betrayed. So we ran and made a choice that would change us forever. It may have been a choice that seemed to be your only hope or option at the time, but desperation doesn't make sound choices.

Hagar's flight to the desert left her at a spring beside the road. The angel of the Lord met her there and told her to return to Sarai and submit to her authority. After that encounter with God, Hagar gave God a new name. She called him *El Roi*, "The God Who Sees Me" (see Gen. 16:11–15), the very God David is beginning to understand himself in Psalm 139.

God's Word beckons us to gird up in His power and strength and confront the past. He calls us to share our losses and pain with Him, and to realize He has already seen it all. Why? Why share our wounds, painful losses, or horrible decisions from the past with a God who already knows it all? Because inviting Jesus into your pain and secrets allows God to use all of our past for all of our freedom and His kingdom. An unstuck past allows Him to completely heal us and move us into His complete kingdom plan.

Unstuck Truth #7: Sometimes we have to go back to get ahead.

More times than not, our past weighs us down, keeping us from an unstuck life. It dictates what we believe about the present, our pessimism for the future, our inability to expect anything good. However, hope awaits when we understand God wants to use *everything* we have gone through to bring us the peace, purpose, and passion He desires for us.

I understand this may be a new concept for you. Much secular counseling often stresses that the primary key to changing lives is discovering and uncovering repressed memories, buried trauma, and damaging messages from our childhood in order to *get past* the past. Basically, this theory of thought says, "If you know where you are coming from, you can know where to go next and even change your direction." But God operates differently. God says *remember*.

Remember . . . the days of your youth. (Eccles. 12:1)

Sometimes, without realizing it, we paralyze our purpose in Christ, our assignments, and our calling by holding on to or covering up what is in the past. It is not even always the *bad* things that keep us stuck. Sometimes it is our former successes that keep us from taking risks and trusting God. We girls have to avoid the Scarlett O'Hara syndrome—"I'll think about that tomorrow." Skipping the lessons God has for us in healing the past sets us up for remaining *stuck* in unlearned lessons, unsolved issues, and unresolved grief.

God wants to use our broken, restored past for present and future life unstuck.

Six Reasons for Going Back to Get Ahead

1. God heals what is revealed.

Healing the past begins with sharing your story with someone you trust. You will be amazed at what this step alone does to set you free. The Bible says in James 5:16 that when we share our past, our sins, and our heartbreak, we begin the healing process to life unstuck.

2. Covering up versus cleaning up leads to stuck.

I love what John Trent says about this:

Those who are able to honestly and courageously deal with the past as a learning and shaping tool will take the road that leads to authentic living. That's a way of life that enables us to honestly accept ourselves for who we are, warts, weaknesses and all.[1]

3. We pass on what we have not cleaned up.

H. Norman Wright says in his book *Making Peace with Your Past*,

We must consider the importance of the past and recognize the role it plays in the future and what it may be able to tell you about yourself. In your passage through life, you want to be fully in charge of the route, the events, the destination; in order to do so, you need a clear view of where you have been.[2]

4. The Holy Spirit gives us the strength to make peace with our past.

Many times we think just surviving past circumstances and traumas is enough and revisiting those old wounds will be too difficult to endure. But I love what Rebecca St. James said in *The Merciful Scar*, "You were strong enough to survive the real trauma. You're strong enough to let God bring you through the healing, too."[3]

5. Biblical truth is the key to life unstuck.

The truth contained in the Bible transforms us, but we also need to know there is another *reason* God gave us His Word.

The Bible is not an end in itself, but a means to bring men to an intimate and satisfying knowledge of God, that they may enter into Him, that they may delight in His Presence, may taste and know the inner sweetness of the very God Himself in the core and center of their hearts.[4]

6. Freedom comes from surrender.

Allow this journey of looking backward to be the way God begins His amazing healing in your life. Remember, sister, God has not invited you on this journey to abandon you. God never left Hagar; He sent His angels to redirect her path of going back to get ahead. Maybe this book is your angel. I pray it is so.

God never left David, even in the depths of his sin and unrepentance; God never condemned Paul for his past; God has never left me and has brought me through painful places into beautiful freedom and purpose. Trust in the same God; trust He will not leave you alone nor leave you as you are. God invites you to allow Him to help you remember your past, every painful decision and detail, for the purpose of your healing and your freedom. And when you do allow God to repair your past wounds, you will see the fences He put up to ultimately keep you from going down the wrong path.

. . . .

Download "6 Reasons to Weed" from life-unstuck.com.

8

UNSTUCK
Memories

If I go up to the heavens, you are there; if I make my bed in the depths, you are there.

Psalm 139:8

I'll Go First . . .

I grew up in an average home with a mother and father who had married young in rural Savannah, Georgia. My parents stayed married for more than fifty years until my dad died—that was nearly ten years ago. They were blue-collar, God-fearing folk. I have three younger sisters and lots of memories, both good and bad. My parents also came from fairly average American families—neatly woven on the outside but fairly messed up underneath. Their family backgrounds included alcoholism, tobacco and drug addiction, pornography, divorce, adultery, and teen pregnancy. This legacy affected their childhoods and mine. I've learned that family "junk" goes back to Adam and Eve and is truly God's specialty. He uses our personal junk to bring us to good and healed places. My teenage immorality led to a teenage marriage, teenage motherhood, eventual abandonment, and, finally, to becoming a single teenage mother of one precious son. With the help of my parents, I cared for my son and also returned to school. It was in college that I met the next "man of my dreams." The two of us continued in the lifestyle we had both grown accustomed to in the seventies and soon found ourselves with an unplanned pregnancy. The good news was that we were in love and engaged to be married when we found ourselves pregnant. The bad news was that even though I was "in love" and had agreed to be married, I was not "in trust." I had already been left all alone holding a swaddled babe wrapped in a blanket. I was not about to go that route again.

While in college, I had stepped into the butterfly (want to be part of the crowd) and bumblebee (want to be heard and seen) parts of my personality and took hold of the popular Woman's Liberation rhetoric on the college campus. As little as I really knew about the topic, I passionately joined the battle and fought boldly and diligently for "a woman's right to choose." During those days, I could wax eloquent about why women should have a right to determine when and if they wanted to have a child. I proclaimed that we ultimately should "control our own bodies." I was so convincing that my pro-choice opinions were even published in a local woman's newspaper.

When I discovered I was pregnant, just prior to my wedding day, I made what I thought was a logical and healthy decision to abort. As far as I was concerned, my future husband had no vote. He silently obliged me—a choice we would both live to regret. My first visit was to a newly opened neighborhood abortion clinic I deemed dirty and dark, and left without using their services. That abortion facility left such a nasty taste in my mouth I decided to approach my own ob-gyn, the one who had delivered my firstborn son, to obtain the "safe" abortion I had fought so hard to legalize.

Just like my future husband, my ob-gyn never questioned my decision. He simply set the date for two weeks after my wedding day. Yep—some things we do are truly just too stupid to explain. A marriage certificate meant little to me in terms of a man staying for the long haul. My husband and I went on our honeymoon pregnant, with a date for an abortion on our calendars soon after we returned. It was not the honeymoon of every little girl's dreams. Neither was the marriage, not for a very long time.

We had planned to drop our son off at kindergarten and arrive at the hospital at 7:00 a.m. (My husband had already begun the steps to adopt my son.) I paid the extra money to be put to sleep during the abortion procedure, and even with that, we were told the "procedure" would only take "a few minutes." We planned to pick up our son at school, go get some lunch, and move on with life. The abortion would join many other bad choices I had made in my youth and be our secret.

I woke up from the "procedure" unable to move or speak. I had a tube stuck down my throat and a machine breathing for me. While my husband and parents stood at the foot of my hospital bed, the doctor explained I had had an allergic reaction to the anesthesia used to put me to sleep during the abortion. My breathing had stopped during surgery. I had to be admitted to the hospital. My new husband was forced to call my parents to pick up my son from school. I can still remember the look on the faces of my mom and dad as they stood at the foot of my hospital bed. Shock. Shame. Fear. Loss. My secret was a secret no longer.

My feelings of embarrassment, shame, and even anger followed me out of that hospital. They did not leave me for seven long years. My parents never said the word *abortion*. I never said the word. My husband never said the word. What happened closed the casket of my heart and affected my life forever. Whether or not you have ever had an abortion, or even have sexual immorality in your past, it is likely that in some area of your life this "casket of your heart" image will ring true. We all pretty much have some heart caskets.

The reason I share my story is the hope that my transparent sharing will stir and encourage you to begin taking any needed steps toward an unstuck past.

As we talked about in the last chapter, Hagar was a woman not completely unlike you and me, a woman who trusted God and braved a return to her painful past. In the process, she discovered a new identity for God and established her own relationship with Him. She recognized Him as *El Roi*, the God Who Sees!

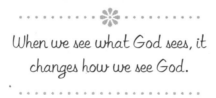

When we see what God sees, it
changes how we see God.

Have I Seen the God Who Sees Me?

Hagar knew beyond any shadow of a doubt that God had *truly* seen her, and from there on out she would always hold on to that truth. We can learn some things from Hagar and from her pain.

Hagar didn't hide how much she was hurt, she didn't cover it up, she didn't try to ignore it. Hagar *embraced* it. Yes, I know. Embracing the pain hurts, I get that. I have faced that. Many times the pain goes too deep and too wide to even begin thinking about embracing it, but hang in there. There is hope. You see, when Hagar embraced her pain, her disappointment, and her circumstances and cried out to God, she came face-to-face with the God who longed to rescue her. That is so amazing I think we need to reread that.

Unstuck Truth #8: When we turn to God with the pain of our past, we are met by the God who has plans for our future.

Remember, the only reason I can state that with such confidence is because I have cried out to God countless times in my pain and suffering. And each time I cry out, I am met by a rescuing God who never stops seeing me!

A Response of Panic Equals a Life of Secrets

We all have things in our past we are not proud of, and some of us have some parts we wish we could escape altogether. However, God wants us to embrace our past, each and every nasty, dirty, hurtful aspect of it. Remember what we said in the last chapter? God heals what is revealed. Let me explain this. If we have not confronted the past in a healthy way, allowing God full control over how He wants to use it in our present and future, we cannot truly experience life unstuck. The fact is, many of us have learned to accommodate our past: we live with it or ignore it, we justify it, live in fear of it, hide it, or let it take over every part of us. What we fail to realize, more often than not, is each of those responses to our past, in essence, has the potential to keep us *stuck* somewhere and somehow from all that God has in mind for us.

Although we may hide our wounds and shame from the rest of the world, we cannot hide from God. Each wound you incurred matters to God and He sees each gash, each cut, each broken bone. The wonderful truth is that God wants to heal your wounds and heal them completely. He wants your life unstuck in every way—past, present, and future. However, God will not force your response. You must reveal your desire and willingness for Him to heal. And this is our biggest obstacle: our willingness to be healed.

Let's go back to Hagar for a bit. Anyone would agree she had incurred some painful wounds from both Abram and Sarai, right? We don't know each and every word spoken, pot slammed, huff and puff given, or dirty glance fired, but we too are women. We know how painful it is when your dreams are shattered and promises broken, right? We also know how easy it is to run away from our problems, and many times we do, but Hagar didn't run too long before crying out in her desperation. This is where many of us, including me, may stop the healing journey. This is where we get stuck. We are afraid of that choking, gasping, coughing, crying bit where our hearts feel permanently lodged in our throats. You know, when the snot flows freely and mingles with the barrage of tears we cannot stop; when the world ceases to turn and all joy seems to vanish right before our eyes? When we relive the pain and the abuse, and the fears and anger return, and we want to scream and hide all at the same time? There. Right there. That is where God finds you. That is when the rescuing God *who sees you* saves you. That is when God tells you how He never stopped loving you, weeps with you, holds you tightly, and promises to never let you go as He begins to heal what you reveal to Him.

There is no question about it. God is a saving God. He wants to do it; He wants to rescue you. He wants to save you from your pain. He wants to heal you. And you know what else God wants to do? He wants to take all of your pain and suffering, each excruciating part of your past, and turn it into something beautiful for His glory and for your ministry. Whoa! That is so like our God, isn't it? To take something horrible and turn it into something not only useful, but *beautiful*. I love how the Bible puts this very idea in Isaiah 61, which tells us that Jesus was sent to heal the brokenhearted, to comfort our mourning and grief, and to exchange all that heartbreak and shame for praise and purpose.

God promises to exchange our pain for His purpose, if we allow Him. This very idea has brought me endless encouragement throughout the years as I have believed this truth and acted upon it. Yes, it is frustrating to know I cannot keep myself from pain and trials, but I can rest assured knowing "that in all things God works for the good of those who love him, who have been called according to his purpose" (Rom. 8:28).

Praise God, right? He can make all things good, regardless of how much they hurt to begin with. But you know what else? I also realized through the years that the way God gets the most glory from my painful past is when I share it, verbally, with others. Yes, when I, Pat Layton, share with others what He has brought me through, He does the work in not only getting *me* unstuck through the act of sharing but also in encouraging others to trust Him to get *them* unstuck as well. Dear sister, I am here to encourage you to take hold of every ounce of the freedom God offers you, and in that, to share what God has done for you and through you, and how He has redeemed and rescued you, with a world that so desperately needs hope.

I bet I know what is going through your heart and mind right now. I bet you are feeling a bit fearful and anxious about sharing. Can I lay it on the line for you? God's enemy, Satan, wants nothing more than to keep us feeling worthless, feeling guilty, or feeling as though we have nothing "powerful" to share; he wants to keep us silent and hiding our secrets. It is time to break the power of secrecy over our lives and believe God wants to show you life unstuck. He wants to heal you and set you free! As you begin to trust God's heart toward you regarding your freedom, you will also notice one more beautiful aspect of God's tenderness toward you, His beloved daughter:

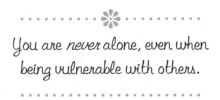

You are *never* alone, even when being vulnerable with others.

You see, God designed us ladies, and men too for that matter, for strong relationships. We were meant to grasp hands and hearts with others and share pain together. You may have witnessed first-hand what happens when two or more people intentionally do this: God shows up. God does amazing things with people who are humble and open to His supernatural surgery of hearts. Dear sister, we were never intended to struggle alone. It is through the community of Christ-followers we learn to heal. It is through this same community we learn God's truth. It is through community we learn what God has done for others. And it is through community others learn what God has done for and through you. And though the very thought of being "exposed" or "found out" may terrify you, let me assure you God's desire is not to expose you and leave you feeling alone and vulnerable. Quite the contrary! God's very nature is to protect and care for you, His daughter, and He covers His children with grace, *never* with shame.

So, under the protection of Almighty God, and in the covering of His unending love and acceptance, tell your story. Tell your sisters how you have been set free from your fear. Declare how your Father saved you from your distress and anguish. Shout from the rooftops how your mighty God turned the ashes of your life into something altogether beautiful. Glorify God through the pain, knowing how that pain can indeed set you free . . . and give your sisters the hope they can be set free, and free indeed, as well.

Share, declare, shout, proclaim, and do it today—get unstuck from the past.

. . . .

Visit life-unstuck.com to download the free "Freedom Flower" life mapping tool and for additional help for your "going back to get ahead" life unstuck journey.

9

UNSTUCK
Faith

If I rise on the wings of the dawn, if I settle on the far side
of the sea.

Psalm 139:9

I stretched across my daughter's curled up, sleeping, hoodie-
covered body from my middle seat on the airplane and
took a look out the window. She never moved. My husband
snored, not so softly, on my other side. Most everyone on the filled
airplane did the same. It was close to two a.m. as we were pressing
through the last miles of our journey from the east (Florida) to the
west (Alaska). I don't sleep very well on airplanes, but at this late
hour and after an exhausting day of travel, even I was slipping in
and out of dreamland. It was early January and my foggy thoughts
vacillated between *What the heck was I thinking?* and *Just how far
is the east from the west?* How in heaven's name did I end up on

an airplane traveling from a beautiful, sunny, wintertime Florida, the land to which birds and humans flock, to Alaska, the land in which nothing survives in the middle of January?

I clearly remembered the timeline of my journey. I had been speaking at an event the previous October when a woman came up to me afterward and said, "God told me to bring you to Alaska." "Cool," I responded. "I love to travel and speak and I have never been to Alaska. I have always wanted to visit during the summer, but my distaste for flying has kept me away. It's a long flight."

"Oh no," she said, "I want you to come in January! Next January."

January? In Alaska? You have got to be kidding. There is no way I am flying to Alaska in January, was what I thought. What I said was, "Well, we will have to see. My calendar fills up pretty quickly . . . have your people call my people and we'll talk." I quoted her some ridiculous fees and expectations, hugged her, and walked away thinking I'd never hear from her again. God, however, had a different plan.

I arrived back home from the conference to find her message waiting. She had gone back to Alaska and talked to "her people." They said *yes* to all of my silly requests and added that they would pay my husband's and daughter's way too, as well as put us up in a beautiful B&B for a week of bear hunting, I mean "sightseeing," in Alaska, in January.

Oh my. "I'll have to pray about it and talk to my husband," I told her.

I prayed. God said go.

I talked to my husband. He said yes.

I prayed again. God still said go.

I packed my ski jacket and lots of long underwear, got on a plane, and headed for Alaska in January.

Hence, my stretching across my daughter to look out the airplane window at two a.m., 10,000 feet in the air, at *zero* minus whatever number degrees. I am telling you right now, I got on that airplane utterly afraid. My family slept the entire flight. I prayed the entire flight. I cried out to God in the quiet of that airplane and reminded Him (and myself) over and over and over how my trust was in Him and not airplanes.

What I have discovered about unstuck fear is that there is only one solution, one surefire and 100-percent-guaranteed way to overcome fear. That one thing is *faith*.

As we began to slow for our approach into Fairbanks, Alaska, I looked out onto the snow-covered mountains reaching mightily and aggressively toward heaven to touch the full moon-and star-filled sky. I lost my breath at the wonder of what I was seeing. All I could think was *Alaska glows*. I was absolutely awestruck. I honestly cannot wrap words around that scene. I have never, and may never again, see anything like it in my lifetime. The majesty and wonder that filled my heart at that moment were indescribable. I can recall only a few slightly comparable times in my life to rival it. I have often wondered about the verse that says God has flung our sins away as far as the "east is from the west," and I couldn't help but think of that verse as I was literally about as far as the east from the west in flying from Florida to Alaska.

 **Unstuck Truth #9:** Grief looks down, fear looks around, faith looks up!

It is too easy to run into the wilderness of fear, shame, abandonment, anger, or self-protection only to find ourselves *stuck* and not really living the life of our dreams. God has a better plan, but we have to trust Him with our past and even believe He is able to sift the bad stuff of our past and use it all for good. Beth Moore reminds us, in her beautiful study of Esther, that there is treasure in your past that God wants to put square in the middle of your future. Contrary to what you might think or feel, just like Esther, God has chosen you for a specific purpose—not in spite of your history but because of it. God never wastes a woman who is willing, but oftentimes our hope for life unstuck is stuck in our fear of the unknown. Stuck in places we are not willing to go. Stuck in our lack of faith and trust in the God who *can* do in us and through us what we can *never* do outside of Him.

Philippians 2:13 says something along the lines of "God is working in you to help your *want to* become *willing to*." Are you willing to want to go back and see what might be the hidden key for your life today that was left in your past?

One of the first verses I felt God bring alive in my heart was Jeremiah 1:5, "Before I formed you in the womb I knew you, before you were born I set you apart."

I remember the two sides of my heart upon first reading those words. My first thought was for the unborn child I had destroyed. I was so tenderly aware of how God forms each life in the womb and has a specific plan for him or her. Once I was able to recover from my own travailing cries of repentance and heartbreak over that truth, I was able to take hold of it for myself and realize: God not only formed and knew my baby but He formed and knew me. God had set me apart as well and was fully aware of the wrong turns I would take and the need for me to stop going in the direction I was heading and turn around toward Him.

God has set us each apart for a special work designed specifically for our mix of personality quirks. A work no one else can do but us. The Bible says in 1 Peter 4:11, "If anyone ministers, let [her] do it as with the ability which God supplies" (NKJV).

Think about this special work planned by God for these special people before time began:

God knew Israel would need some rules and regulations, so He designed Moses with a love for law and order.

God knew He would need a fiery advocate who knew where grace meets sin, so He designed Paul.

God knew some women would buy the slimy enemy lie of abortion and desperately need to hear of His redeeming love, so God made *me*.

What do you think might be part of the special assignment God has in mind for your life?

God Searches for Those Who Are Lost

In the last chapter, we talked about the power found in sharing our story. In fact, Scripture tells us that powerful ministry results from "the word of [our] testimony" (Rev. 12:11). The thing is, we have to be *willing* to go the distance with God, to be cleaned up, inside and out, so He can get glory from our story and put us in places where that story needs to be heard, even if it is Alaska in the dead of winter.

As I shared earlier, I thought my choice for abortion was my key to freedom and instead I found myself stuck and in pain, shame, and loss—most of which I didn't even understand. My husband and I lived in various levels of that pain for the next seven years. We battled lack of trust, fear of abandonment, and shame along with the inability to communicate and share our loss. We were two broken people who had no clue how to fix our pain or how to save our marriage. If you recall, my husband had taken the legal steps to adopt my son immediately after signing our marriage papers, and we soon became pregnant with our next son. I think we both secretly hoped that by having a child so soon after we married we would somehow heal from the deadly choice we had made. And in many ways God did use our sons to save us.

My husband was very determined, regardless of how miserable he was, that divorce was not an option. He had grown up in a broken home and did not want that for our sons. Although we separated a few times, we always "somehow" came back together.

Our marriage was on its very last thread when our oldest son, Tim, celebrated his birthday. My husband, Mike, decided to celebrate with Tim by inviting two other dads and their sons to go on a weekend canoeing and camping trip. They chose to load up the canoes and paddle as far from civilization as they could in one day. After a full day of canoeing, they arrived at their desired camping spot in the middle of the woods. The dads released their sons to go for a swim while they set up the campsite and prepared for dinner. The boys had barely stepped away when bloodcurdling screams came from the water's edge. The men ran toward their boys and the boys ran toward their dads . . . all three covered with blood from head to toe. Our own Tim's blood. Tim had dived into the water and hit his head on an underwater tree stump. His head was cut open from back to front.

They were in the middle of nowhere.

The men began to wrap Tim's head in all the fabric they could gather. Then they loaded him and the other boys back into the canoes and started the long journey back toward help. When they finally arrived at an interstate connection, they climbed up the hill from the river to flag down help. Get the picture here: three men and three boys covered in blood and dirt, hitchhiking on the side of the interstate. Two little old ladies (angels in the desert) stopped and loaded Mike and Tim into the back of their car. A few hours and an ambulance ride later, we were given the grim news. Not only had Tim ripped open his scalp but he had in fact also broken his neck in three places. God Himself had carried Tim up out of that river, back down the long path, and to the hospital for care.

Tim spent the next three months in "halo" traction, but recovered fully from his injuries. "Halo" is right!

While that was all happening in our lives, at the same time God was orchestrating our eternal rescue. You see, Tim's accident was just a few weeks before Easter. God used every single bit of that experience to lead us to a newfound faith in Him. That Easter our entire family got a fresh introduction to the suffering sacrifice of Jesus as He chose to shed His precious blood for us. The nails in Tim's head allowed us a firsthand reality of the pain and suffering Jesus endured for our redemption and life unstuck.

John 10:10 says this:

> The thief does not come except to steal, and to kill, and to destroy. I have come that they may have life, and that they may have it more abundantly. (NKJV)

God showed us through that experience with Tim how we are *never* too far from Him. We are never out of His sight or off His mind. He longs to have our hearts, minds, and souls so that He can take what has been broken, fix it up, and use it in His big plan.

Unstuck Desires

I have learned that women have four basic needs that are critical for life unstuck:

1. *Control.* Yes, I said control. Admit it. We girls like to be in charge: in charge of the husband, in charge of the kids, in charge of the house, in charge of the church. It's every woman's battle. It started with the very first woman God created, in the Garden of Eden . . . it started with Eve! The thing is, God *did* create Eve. He knew her as she was being formed. He designed her. He knew what was in her and what would come out of her. God desired for Eve to have dominion, not demands. God gave Eve "control" over her environment to make her life full—abundant—unstuck. Eventually, it is that "control" we crave that God demands we surrender. I *first* surrendered control just after Tim's accident. I have since

surrendered it many times (can you spell A-L-A-S-K-A?) and I will certainly be required to surrender some more. Unstuck control leads to life unstuck.

2. *Consideration.* Women need to feel valued, noticed, chosen. We have an innate need for purpose and a place in the world. In our own strength, that desire always leads to death. God has a place and a purpose for each of us, but first we have to surrender our way of finding that place and purpose and allow God to show us *His.* As a young college student, I fought for my voice. I fought for the attention and "rights" that God was longing to lead me into. Ultimately, you and I can only find that beautiful consideration in God's plans and love.

3. *Companionship.* We were created as creatures of connection. We are not meant to be isolated in body, mind, or spirit. Consider the most vulnerable position for any enemy attack: alone and undefended. God's plan is for us to live in community—His community. To start with our hearts and minds focused on Him, then allowing Him to lead us to those people and places, will keep us unstuck and protected.

   David says, "If I rise on the wings of the dawn, if I settle on the far side of the sea"(Ps. 139:9). He sees that God is in fact the 3-D God we talked about in chapter 1. He is *there.* He is, and desires to be, your constant companion. He wants to fill your life with others who understand that kind of love. "Two can stand back-to-back and conquer" (Eccles. 4:12 NLT).

4. *Contentment.* We need to have our needs met. We need to experience peace, purpose, and passion. We need life unstuck. But we need to see what God sees and believe what God believes. Only then can we find true contentment, because only then are we finding our contentment in the only One who will never disappoint—our Lord.

This is the thing about living life unstuck: we have to do it uncomfortably and at times afraid. We have to do it by faith. God will settle for nothing less. If we are going to embrace peace with the past in order to be used 100 percent by God in the present and future, we have to face our fears and deal with some stuff. We have to embrace every morsel of faith we can scrounge up and trust God *completely*.

"If I rise on the wings of the dawn, if I settle on the far side of the sea," even there, Lord, you will find me.

God made you for a specific calling, probably a few specific callings.

Look behind you, friend; your unstuck freedom may be hiding back there.

. . . .

Visit life-unstuck.com for a free downloadable "Desires of an Unstuck Woman" life balance wheel.

10

UNSTUCK
Freedom

Even there your hand will guide me, your right hand will hold me fast.

Psalm 139:10

Sometimes it is not easy to live with women! I grew up always being referred to as "the oldest daughter" in a home with three younger sisters. We could go from cat fight to best friends in a millisecond. There were times in our home when you could not tear us girls apart with a crowbar, and then there were those times when crowbars were considered for things that should remain unspoken. We were an emotional roller coaster of girls!

When we were very young, our dad taught all four of us how to water ski. You might imagine the amount of patience that took. We would go out in our family boat and would each take our turn around the lake as many times as we could without falling. Once you fell your turn was over, and another sister was waiting to jump in and take your place. If I fell too soon, before I was ready to give my turn up, I would struggle with all of my might to grab that ski rope back and try again before another sister jumped into the water to take my spot. I would gather up all the eight-year-old strength I could muster to get that rope back into my hands. I would flounder and struggle in the water with all that gear attached to me: a life jacket the size of a small car and water skis reaching a mile high, crisscrossing throughout my struggle. I would just get exhausted trying to get to the rope in time to not lose my turn.

I can remember my dad calling out to me, "Pat, just relax. Lie back on your life jacket and I will bring the rope to you!" And he would. I would rest in the water and my dad would drive the boat slowly and carefully around me until the ski rope would just float right into my hands. No struggle, no fear of missing it, no one jumping in and taking my place.

In twenty-five years of women's ministry I have often either found myself in a similar situation or watched another sister struggle to grab something she was afraid she might lose—a ministry spot, a child, a husband, maybe another friend. Sometimes, we feel that if we don't struggle and strive, we will lose our "turn." We are afraid that somehow what God has called us to do has been or will be missed or that another sister might jump in and take our spot. When those times come in my life, I try to remember my dad's words: "Pat, just let the rope come to you."

I love the words in this verse that remind us God is quite capable of "bringing the rope to us." He is more than capable of guiding and directing our path into His plans, when we relax and allow Him to do so.

As I have led women on the healing journey toward an unstuck past, I have discovered two dangerous places for getting stuck in the past:

1. Hanging on to unresolved anger and shame.
2. Gripping misconceptions about forgiveness, both for themselves and others.

In this chapter, I want us to be reminded beyond any shadow of a doubt that God's got us! He *will* guide this journey and He *will* hold us tightly while we take hold of it.

Unstuck Truth #10: God's grip reveals God's grace as God guides.

When our past has left us hurt and those wounds are not tended to in a healthy manner, resentment, anger, and bitterness remain embedded in the soil of our hearts until they are taken care of through God's redemptive healing power.

Unstuck Anger

Take a moment to let God's truth empower you. Are you ready to be empowered? OK, here it is:

Go ahead and be angry. You do well to be angry—but don't use your anger as fuel for revenge. (Eph. 4:26 Message)

Did you read that? God says to go ahead and get angry! Embrace your anger just as you embrace your pain. Feel it. Don't run away from it. Anger is a wonderful tool. It keeps us aware of injustice being done to others so we can rise to someone's defense, and sometimes even moves us to repentance.

The problem here is not anger. The problem is how we deal with it. When we use any emotion improperly, we can damage others and ourselves. Unhealthy emotions keep us *stuck*. A huge part of our journey toward life unstuck comes from learning how to handle our emotions properly.

In Matthew 21:10–13 we find a story about Jesus going to worship the Father and being met by myriads of temple businessmen cheating and extorting the people who were there to worship. These men were conducting business in the outer courts, which just happened to be the only place Gentiles were allowed to worship. So not only were they cheating and extorting the Jews but they were also preventing the Gentiles from worshiping God. No wonder Jesus got angry. He had every right to be incensed at their actions, and His holy and righteous anger drove the wicked away so the people could once more approach the Father in spirit and in truth. This was anger used appropriately.

The Bible gives us many examples of what can happen when anger is *not* dealt with God's way.

Moses's anger over the treatment of a Hebrew slave led him to kill an Egyptian.

Peter's anger over Jesus being arrested led him to seize a sword and cut off a servant's ear.

Cain's anger that his sacrifice wasn't accepted led him to kill his brother Abel.

The Bible also shows us a good number of examples of how people became angry and dealt with it in healthy ways.

Queen Esther's anger over how her people were to be killed led her to expose the source of the persecution, Haman.

Nathan's anger at David's sin with Bathsheba led him to confront David, which led to his repentance.

Paul's anger at Peter because of his hypocritical actions toward the Gentiles in the presence of the Jews led to Peter's repentance and Paul being sent to declare the gospel to the Gentiles.

Each circumstance is different, because each circumstance had a different reason for the anger.

Anger is almost always rooted within other emotions: fear, betrayal, injustice, or selfish ambition, for example, with the main two being betrayal or frustration due to blocked goals. When you get mad and those feelings start to bubble up, threatening to take control and take over, take a deep breath and realize your anger must be handled quickly, but carefully and healthily. When the goal of expressing our anger is to help others, help our relationships, and help ourselves, we are well on our way. We would also do well to read the rest of that verse's context—you know, the one about getting angry?

> And don't stay angry. Don't go to bed angry. Don't give the Devil that kind of foothold in your life. (Eph. 4:27 Message)

Confronting unresolved and often unidentified anger is vital to life unstuck. In fact, we cannot enjoy all that God has for our peace, purpose, and passion without dealing with *all* anger and unforgiveness we carry. Talk about being stuck. Unresolved emotions are heavy, heavy, heavy! So, how do we get unstuck from the emotions that often follow a look back into the past? How do we forgive that horrible wrong done to the little girl we once were? How do we stop striving to please that unpleasable boyfriend who left us so long ago? How do we forgive that cheating husband so that love can be rediscovered? How do we get un-angry when we have such good reason to stay mad?

We unstick forgiveness.

Unstuck Forgiveness

I have often heard unresolved anger and unforgiveness likened to drinking poison and expecting the other person to die. Many of us wrongly assume that if we forgive someone's actions done to us we are, in essence, saying what they did is acceptable and we are allowing ourselves to continue to be their doormat.

Nothing could be further from the truth. I share these truths in my book *A Surrendered Life*:

> Forgiveness is a process, and it is a continual one, where we recognize we have been wronged but we place the burden of resentment and justice in God's hands—We give the rope to Him!
>
> Forgiveness does NOT mean we forget, like some type of weird spiritual amnesia, but we choose to no longer hold that offense against our offender. It is the same way God interacts with us. When the Bible says God "will no longer remember [our] sins," it means God does not catalog them and use our past sins against us. He asked the same of us for others.
>
> Forgiveness does not water down the offense by trivializing it. It is embracing the truth that you were hurt and possibly hurt quite badly. Forgiveness calls the violation what it is: an offense, and leaves a just God to enact justice.[1]

Life unstuck depends upon three powerful words: "I forgive you." Is there anything more beautiful than those three little words? Even "I love you" pales in comparison, because wrapped up within forgiveness is love, acceptance, and reconciliation. Forgiveness is the lynchpin upon which freedom, healing, and purpose rest. Anger is incredibly difficult and exhausting to work through, but forgiving others lightens our load as we continue our journey toward life unstuck. Many of us have heard about forgiveness, especially in a church setting. We know about Jesus's words on the cross: "Father, forgive them, for they do not know what they are doing"(Luke 23:34). You may have even heard friends or family members speak about how God has forgiven them, or experienced forgiveness through Jesus's death on the cross for yourself. However, many of us know *nothing* about the power of forgiving others. Why?

We think, when we are stuck there, that we can protect ourselves from ever being hurt again, but that is a lie the enemy uses to keep us from our calling, our anointing, and our assignments. We can forgive the offender or we can let the offense be another heavy weight in the muddy places of life that keeps us stuck. The devil wants you to stay stuck in unforgiveness, anger, and fear. He *likes* you stuck right there.

It's exciting, actually, if we stop striving for control and the last word. Oh my, what God can do to lavish unstuck freedom on our lives if we let Him!

Forgiving Yourself

I have something to say here that may rock your stuck place about forgiving yourself. Trust me, I get this. I have lived with the choice to destroy my own innocent, unborn child. I have lived with immoral choices I made in my youth. I have lived with some bad parenting I wish I could redo. I have lived with some friendship mistakes that can never be undone. And on and on and on. We all have made and will make mistakes.

As women, we often feel that while God has forgiven us, we cannot seem to forgive ourselves. This is my big announcement, my friend, a truth that once realized will leave you with life unstuck forever:

God never intended for us to forgive ourselves.

The Bible does not identify the need to forgive ourselves. In fact, I don't think we are capable of it. When we try to forgive ourselves we seek to do God's work in His place. The very heart of the gospel is not forgiving yourself but accepting God's forgiveness.

It's Your Choice

True forgiveness is not a feeling but rather an *unstuck choice*.

Forgiveness is an act of obedience to God and an act of surrender that will allow His full blessing on your life as you release the entanglement of holding on to unforgiveness.

When we forgive a person, he or she is permanently forgiven. We are to forgive the same way that God forgives: supernaturally, permanently, and unconditionally. When you have asked God to forgive you, you are permanently forgiven. Satan wants to keep us stuck in unforgiveness and anger. When he tries to drag you back down and make you think that you haven't really forgiven someone, or that you are not really forgiven, you just speak right back at him the words of truth you have captured.

Unstuck peace with the past is an amazingly powerful weapon for living life unstuck. When we forgive, when we release all anger, when we express ourselves by healthy means, we experience life unstuck and are free to soar so God can take us places we never dreamed possible!

My sweet friend, I know this is not an easy step. I have taken it myself. I understand how difficult it is to even consider forgiving others, knowing the heartbreak some of us have endured. I have held many, many women in my arms as they have made the brave choice to give God the rope and allow Him to handle their heartaches. He takes these wounds tenderly into His capable hands.

Forgiving is God's territory, not ours—both for those we need to forgive and for forgiving ourselves, His forgiveness is a gift. Give it. Accept it. Get unstuck from unforgiveness, right here. Right now.

11

UNSTUCK
Light

If I say, "Surely the darkness will hide me and the light become night around me."

Psalm 139:11

Fighting the Night with the Light

When our two oldest grandsons were both tiny boys, we went on a camping trip to Walt Disney World with some other families from our church. After a long day of boy-filled camping, we all settled into the darkness of the camper. After the normal amount of scuffling and boy noises, we were all drifting off to a sweet sleep when suddenly my husband jumped up out of bed, practically throwing me onto the floor, whipping his blanket around and yelling. Both grandsons immediately responded by jumping out of their beds, and panic took hold of four hundred square feet of camping space. It turned out a mouse (I know—it *was* Disney) had scurried across our bed! Oh my. When we finally got the lights on, everyone was standing on something and no one was willing to go back to sleep with that *rodent* running free. But eventually, all the boys gave in to snoring. Me? I plopped myself in the driver's seat of that RV with a flashlight pointed right on my boys in one hand and a pot in the other. If I had to, I was armed and ready to take that critter on for the safety of my G boys. I stayed awake until sunrise, and the park ranger sent a cute little truck with a Mickey Mouse logo to trap that varmint.

In this verse of Scripture David is reminded that God isn't scared of a little darkness: in fact, bring it on!

● ● ● ● ●

As I write this chapter about darkness versus light, God has ruffled my *stuck*. I feel He really wants me to step into this chapter in a fresh way. I have just in the past few minutes received two texts, one from a family member asking for a loan to help her pay rent, and one from a friend who has just received a doctor's confirmation of bladder cancer requiring bladder removal and chemo.

How do I respond to these precious people in my life?

If I say that . . . this might happen. If I say this . . . that might happen.

Oh my, my. What a powerful contemplation, and definitely one I need to experience more often than I do. Think about the power of *one personal question*.

If I say, "You are a bratty child who *never* listens to your mother," what lasting harm have I inflicted upon the heart of my little one?

If I say, "No, I just can't teach that Sunday school class, I am too busy," what opportunity might I miss to change a life?

If I say, "OK, just one drink," what destruction might come upon the rest of my life?

We looked pretty deeply in chapter 4 about the power of our words. We embraced the truth that God knows the way of our say. He knows the words we will say before we say them. The power of words is again on David's heart in verse 11. Let's look at a few different versions of David's internal discussion:

"I could ask . . . " (NLT)

"I said to myself . . . " (Message)

"Suppose I wanted to . . . " (ERV)

David is considering the results of his response. I envy that so much. I want that! With these little words, David is making a choice for light over darkness.

If I say "the darkness will hide me," it will keep me hidden where I am stuck.

In this chapter, I am going to ask you to look for the shadows in your life for the purpose of allowing God to exchange what you have seen and experienced in your past with what He sees and wants to do with your past.

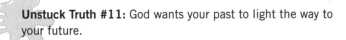

Unstuck Truth #11: God wants your past to light the way to your future.

You see, sister, our freedom hinges upon *the light of the world* illuminating every part of our lives—dispelling all darkness. What exactly is the darkness? Things that have hurt us. Lies we have believed. We have said before how our lives are a mosaic of all our past experiences, both good and bad, right? Think of your life like a gorgeous and intricately complicated work of stained glass. There are pieces of the masterpiece, like the grays and blacks and navies, that we may not like as much as the pinks and yellows and reds, but they are all needed to accurately portray the full picture God is working in us. Remember how we just said God desires to work

117

all of our pain for our good, His glory, and our ministry? In order for God to work all those areas for good and continue to build the stained-glass picture He is creating with our lives, we must allow the light of truth to shine through each and every piece of glass.

Stuck in the Darkness

The first step is to realize we are surrounded by deception. Everywhere we turn we encounter lies, and we are provided an opportunity to either believe them or refute them. Bombarded constantly with multimedia presentations of what we "need" or "should" have in order to be happy, it's a real war zone out there. First of all, did you know there are basically three kinds of "truths" we process as adults? Let me explain.

First, there is "internal truth." Internal truth is what you think or perceive to be true. This is based upon what we have personally experienced and felt: the words we remember being said, the intentions we interpret behind the words said. Our internal truths also include what we *think* the other party thinks. So, internal truth happens internally—in our minds and imaginations—and it is incredibly subjective.

Second, there is "external truth." This is what someone else actually thinks. This is realized by what they say, how they act and react, and what they believe. Remember too that the external truth is dependent upon *their* internal truth. External truth can only be known by listening to what the other person says and gleaned by how they act, *not* by what you assume. The news is external truth . . . it's reporting what other people say. External truth is also very subjective.

Finally, there is "eternal truth." This is God's truth. This is not subjective in the least. It is unwavering, always true, never proven false, and always stands firm, regardless of external or internal circumstances. God's truth is found in God's Word, the Bible.

Mess-ups happen when we rely upon our fickle internal truth to guide us and floundering external truths to persuade us instead of standing firmly established on eternal truth. You see, God's desire is for His truth and His rules to rule our lives and thoughts, and He desires this because it is for our good. So, what does eternal truth say about sin and being stuck?

> Stand fast therefore in the liberty by which Christ has made us free [unstuck], and do not be entangled [stuck] again with a yoke of bondage. (Gal. 5:1 NKJV)

Here are some typical lies that keep women stuck in darkness, among a myriad of others:

I can't help the way I am.

I don't have the time to do everything I'm supposed to do.

I have to have a (husband, new car, great career, child, new home) in order to be happy.

I'm just going through a rebellious stage; it's OK.

I can't control my emotions.

I will never be beautiful.

I'm worthless.

I will never let anyone hurt me again.

I'll never forgive them.

God may forgive me, but I can never forgive myself.

One thing they all have in common? They are all lies. Where did they come from? It doesn't matter if they came from a magazine or television interview, if they were heard from a parent or a friend, if they were said about you or about someone else. Each and every lie is poisonous, and that poison infects our entire heart as we believe the lies. They may not be accepted right away, but they are repeated over and over in ears and hearts until they are believed. Then they are believed over and over until they are acted upon. Finally they are acted upon over and over until they are accepted as truth. It is a vicious cycle. Are you caught in this cycle? Have you been caught in this rut? Do you struggle with these lies? There is hope. First, let's go to the Bible again.

> The LORD detests lying lips,
> but he delights in people who are trustworthy. (Prov. 12:22)

> There are six things the LORD hates,
>   seven that are detestable to him:
>   haughty eyes,
>   a lying tongue,
>   hands that shed innocent blood,
>   a heart that devises wicked schemes,
>   feet that are quick to rush into evil,
>   a false witness who pours out lies
>   and a man who stirs up conflict in the community.
>   (6:16–19)

Yikes! God takes lies seriously. Why do you think He is so adamantly against lying? Because lies lead only to bondage, and we know for a fact God wants to set us free. God has given us laws and guidelines to abide by, not to make us miserable or control us but to protect us by setting healthy boundaries for our own *good*.

Here is the light switch we need, a few truths concerning lies that would be good for us to remember:

1. We have an enemy (1 Pet. 5:8).
2. His greatest tool is deception (2 Cor. 11:3).
3. His favorite tactic is causing us to question God's instructions (Gen. 3:1).
4. He always challenges God's character and goodness (Gen. 3:4).
5. His ultimate goal is broken relationships with God and others (Gen. 3:6).

Considering this, it is not too difficult to assume you have some lies you have believed in your time here on earth, lies that are hindering you from the ultimate and awesome freedom God wants for you. You, now, can relate more personally with David when he wrote:

> When I kept silent about my sin, my body wasted away
> Through my groaning all day long.
> For day and night Your hand was heavy upon me;
> My vitality was drained away as with the fever heat of
> summer.
> I acknowledged my sin to You,
> And my iniquity I did not hide.
> I said, "I will confess my transgressions to the LORD";
> And You forgave the guilt of my sin. (Ps. 32:3–5 NASB)

God longs for you to enjoy unstuck light in every area of your life. He wants you to exchange His light for the darkness the enemy has kept you in: the heartbreak, the secrets, the bad choices, the abuse, the fear, the shame.

God can absolutely shatter it all by one simple "If I say" choice, by the light of His Word. Remember, if we want to experience true and complete unstuck peace with the past, we must be willing to trust the Lord to take us on the unfamiliar and risky path.

We have to choose the light of God's Word instead of darkness.

Yes, it may be scary and yes, you may be very fearful to confront these lies. But you have already tried on your own to make your way out of the darkness, and where has that led you? It has led you right here, with your Rescuer waiting to lead you into all truth and light. So take His hand and acknowledge that you are powerless to heal yourself. Admit you need a Savior who can and wants to rescue you, re-create you, and restore you from the inside out!

Take a minute to consider this unstuck light.

Do you believe God is disappointed with you? The truth is God *delights* in you (Ps. 149:4) and *nothing* can separate us from His love (Rom. 8:37–39).

Do you believe you have done something so horrible it cannot be forgiven? The truth is God forgives *all* our sin when we confess it (1 John 1:9).

Do you believe you are worthless and ugly? The truth of God's Word says we are *radiant* as we look to Christ (Ps. 34:5) and we are God's own possession, chosen for the praise of His glory with an inheritance as His children (Eph. 1:13–14).

What an amazing God we serve, huh? You see, dear girl, when you hold your beliefs up against the light of God's Word, you may realize they are not only a "bit off" but are totally wrong. Praise God! Remember how we said that we have a real enemy who loves nothing more than to convince us to doubt God's view of us and God's goodness? Well, our enemy can be weakened and defeated. How? Light! God's Word has another name: the Sword of the Spirit (Eph. 6:17). It is with this weapon that Satan is defeated, and its light will dispel all darkness in our hearts and minds. When we take the Bible's precious words and hold them dearly and closely to our hearts and minds, when we use those powerful words to confront the old words and phrases and beliefs, the power our enemy has over us weakens and we get *unstuck*. When this happens, our chains break, we are set free, and we allow God's light to fully shine through us and illumine every pore and cell of our being. We then embody our destiny and our identity as being the light of the world, just as Jesus said we are. Wow.

Exchanging Darkness for Light

I once heard a precious story about a father and his daughter, although I don't know if it is true or a fable. This little girl had a precious possession and it went everywhere with her—a strand of dress-up pearls. These pearls went with her to the grocery store and to church. They went with her to the dinner table and to play dates. She frequently talked about her "pearls" to everyone she met, declaring how wonderful they were, and didn't everyone agree? One day, her daddy took her up on his lap and said, "I love you, do you love me?" to which the little girl replied, "Of course I do, Daddy!" Then the daddy said, "If you love me, then you will give me your pearls." Confused, the little girl said, "Daddy, I love you but I cannot give you my pearls. I love them too much!" Her daddy gave her a sweet kiss, told her goodnight, and tucked her in tightly. This exchange went on nightly for a while, and every time the girl responded she would say, "You know I love you, Daddy, but I just can't give you my pearls!" Her daddy never scolded her or wept or tried to coerce her into giving him the pearls, because he wanted to teach her a lesson—a gentle one. One night, after she had been put to bed for a while, she came out of her room, weeping, and rushed into her daddy's lap. Clutching her pearls tightly, she sobbed, "I . . . love (sob) . . . you . . . Daddy (sob) . . . more . . . than . . . my (sob) . . . pearls." And then she shoved her necklace into his hands and clung tightly to her daddy, sobbing at the loss. Her father sweetly kissed away her tears and calmed her down, telling her how much he valued her gift and her expression of love. Then he reached over to the drawer next to the chair and pulled out a beautiful box lined with velvet. He gave his precious daughter the box and told her to open it. Upon opening the box, the little girl gasped, and showered her beloved father with kisses and squeals of delight. What did the box contain? A strand of genuine pearls. The story ends by the father explaining to his daughter how he desired to give her a gift of genuine pearls in exchange for the fake ones, but she couldn't have both. It wasn't until she gave up her counterfeit pearls that she was able to receive the genuine article. In essence, an exchange had to be made, for there is no place for both fake and real at the same time.

In this step to life unstuck, we are talking about the exchange that must be made in our lives. We must choose to exchange the darkness of our past for the light of our future. In order to do that, we must see how God views each part of the exchange and shift our perception to match His.

In chapter 7, I shared six reasons for going back to get ahead. The third reason was that we pass on what we have not cleaned up. God wants to take each and every despair and sorrow, and light our way to healing and hope once more. He wants to exchange our grief for His joy and healing. As God heals your deepest wounds in your innermost being, you will go down paths and byways you never imagined. As we have walked through these verses of Psalm 139, we have considered some dark places of our past, but we move on with the Light of the World who will illuminate every corner and dispel the monsters in the closets. When we collide with the goodness and kindness of God, we discover life unstuck.

Let's enjoy peace with the past and relish unstuck light, shall we?

12

UNSTUCK
Vision

Even the darkness will not be dark to you; the night will shine like the day, for darkness is as light to you.

Psalm 139:12

I shared earlier about growing up in historic Savannah, Georgia. When we girls were little, Girl Scouts were big in Savannah, the birthplace of Juliette Gordon Low—the founder of Girl Scouts. Now I'm not going to get on a roll about how Girl Scouts have changed. I just want to share the story of how the vision of one woman can make a difference in her world.

Juliette Gordon Low, founder of the Girl Scouts of America, was born Juliette Magill Kinzie Gordon on October 31, 1860, in Savannah, Georgia. "Daisy," as she was affectionately called by family and friends, was the second of six children and was a sensitive and talented youngster. Forever interested in the arts, she wrote poems, sketched, wrote and acted in plays, and later became a skilled painter and sculptor. She also had many pets throughout her life, being particularly fond of exotic birds, Georgia mockingbirds, and dogs. To top it all off, Daisy was also known for her great sense of humor. But her talents did not end here. Daisy was very athletic: a strong swimmer, rower, canoer, and tennis player just to name a few. She was also quirky! One of her special skills was standing on her head. She stood on her head every year on her birthday to prove she still could do it, and also celebrated nieces' and nephews' birthdays by doing the same trick. She was married at the age of twenty-six, already mostly deaf from faulty ear infection treatments in one ear, and she became almost completely deaf due to a punctured eardrum from "good luck rice" being thrown into her good ear at her wedding! But she continued her love of travelling throughout the United States, which started with her boarding school experiences. She had a family very involved in varying wars throughout the world, which also introduced her to individuals throughout the United States and abroad desiring to help the youth become self-sufficient and empowered.

In 1912 she founded the Girl Scouts, beginning in her hometown of Savannah, Georgia, after meeting Sir Robert Baden-Powell, the founder of the Boy Scouts and Girl Guides. She desired to teach and build women of courage, confidence, and character in order to make the world a better place. She purposely brought girls of all backgrounds out of their comfortable places into the great outdoors in order to make them self-reliant, resourceful, and ready for active citizenship outside of the home. She even welcomed girls with disabilities into her Girl Scouts in a time when they were typically excluded from many other groups and activities. This was a natural idea to Daisy, who never let severe back pain, deafness, a dissolved marriage, or even breast cancer keep her from enjoying and participating fully in life. She lost her battle with breast cancer in 1927 and her friends honored her by establishing the Juliette Low World Friendship Fund, which finances international projects for Girl Scouts and Girl Guides around the world. Juliette Gordon Low is buried in her beloved Savannah.[1]

I do love that story and heard it many times as a young girl sitting on the very lawns walked upon by "Daisy." One thing that really strikes me about her story is remembering that when she stepped into her vision for Girls Scouts, she was deaf. "Good luck rice" was the final blow to her already impaired hearing. A tiny piece of rice thrown at a wedding celebration found its way into the only good ear Daisy had left. Think about it, my friend: this woman had a choice right then and there. Daisy could have thrown in the towel and lived a life stuck in hopeless despair. Or she could choose light and a life unstuck, allowing the *imagination* God planted in her, the *talents* and *gifts* and *personality*, the *past* that God had navigated her through, to change the entire world.

Juliette Gordon Low changed my life.

It was in moss-dripping heat of Savannah, Georgia, that I sat with my sisters in the sticky grass and learned about character, hard work, perseverance, passion, and how to dream big dreams.

It's All about What You See

Right now, as you look up from this page and take in your surroundings, what do you see? Are you outside somewhere and able to see your children splashing in the pool? Do you see a pile of dishes in the sink? Do you see a toddler finger painting a new masterpiece for the refrigerator? What do you *see*? One thing I can confidently say you see right now, regardless of where you are, who you are next to, and how many kids are running around, is *light*. Think about it. Without a source of light (a lamp, a flashlight, the sun), not much else is seen, is it? Imagine trying to read the words of this page, or a recipe book, or any printed material without light . . . it's impossible. In all the intricacies of how God made you and me and how wonderfully complex our eyes are, God made them work by taking in light in order to perceive what is around us. We can only see in the light. Light is good and provides much comfort, don't you think? Can you remember back to when you were a little girl and how much reassurance a mere night-light could afford you against the monsters under your bed or the unknowns in your closet? We needed to not only know but actually be shown how the light could dispel the darkness and the unknown in our rooms. In the same way, Psalm 139:12 can give us much comfort and reassurance amidst the dark unknowns in our lives.

Remember, there is no darkness in your life that God can't light. In the same way that our actions cannot cover up our heart's intent, in the same way it is impossible to conceal our fears and emotions from God, in the same way God never has us out of His sight—the darkness covers nothing from God. The night conceals many things from us, but nothing can be concealed when it comes to God. God created the night, just as He did the day, and He is glorified in both. His vision is never dimmed nor strained when it comes to how much *light* is on a subject. This is the same God who created the vast cosmos, quasars, nebulae, and black holes. But you and I both know that physical darkness is not what typically concerns us the most, is it? It is not our struggle against physical darkness that leaves us stuck. It is our struggle against the darkness of our thoughts, the darkness of our enemy, and the darkness of the world that leaves us stuck.

Light. It is a beautiful thing. It can be wonderful, but it can also be really harsh. For example, if you have ever experienced the darkness of a movie theater and then walked into the brightness of a midday sun afterward, you know exactly what I am talking about. But whether soft or harsh, light can be a source of hope to weary travelers or a source of warmth from the cold.

Light is defined by Miriam Webster as "something that makes things visible or affords illumination." And light is also talked about in God's Word. Look at these Scriptures for a moment:

And God said, "Let there be light," and there was light. God saw that the light was good, and he separated the light from the darkness. (Gen. 1:3–4)

> The unfolding of your words gives light;
>   it gives understanding to the simple. (Ps. 119:130)

The light shines in the darkness, and the darkness has not overcome it. (John 1:5)

When Jesus spoke again to the people, he said, "I am the light of the world. Whoever follows me will never walk in darkness, but will have the light of life." (John 8:12)

God's Light Is Good

Back in my days of Girl Scout circles in the grass, another part of my adventure was camping along the marsh in the deep darkness of a Coastal Georgia night. In the heat of the summer, we girls would gather in little green tents and giggle and dream and sometimes share "ghost stories." It would be very difficult for a scaredy-cat like me to get to sleep after a few tales of two-headed monsters that liked little green tents for lunch. In fact, the only thing I liked about those inky sleepovers was the lightning bugs. I loved how after just a few minutes of staring into the nighttime sky we would be gleefully disturbed by lightning bugs, aka "fireflies," lighting up the darkness. Little did I know, as a young eight- or nine-year-old, that someday I would be passing the lessons of the lightning bug along. Now I get to enjoy teaching my "G-babies" how to capture a lightning bug in a jar and create a God-charged lantern.

In spite of the delight of a lightning bug, I, for one, truly appreciate man-made light: flashlights, electric lights in my home, search lights, and even firelight.

Light is good, but I can say without question or hesitation—*vision* is better. Unstuck vision is not born of natural light, it is born of God's light!

David declares in Psalm 139:12, "The night will shine like the day, for darkness is as light to you." Oh, those words just make my heart go pitter-patter. Vision—God's vision—makes my heart soar.

> **Unstuck Truth #12:** Having unstuck vision happens in the light of God's truth.

But you are a chosen people, a royal priesthood, an holy nation, God's special possession, that you may declare the praises of him who called you out of darkness into his wonderful light. (1 Pet. 2:9)

> Your word is a lamp to my feet
> and a light to my path. (Ps. 119:105 ESV)

Sister, you and I have been given the Light of the World, Jesus, to lead and guide us on our way—to get us unstuck so we can see the truth. Think of it this way:

· · · · · · · · · · ❊ · · · · · · · · · · ·

The closer you are to Jesus and the more of the Word you have hidden in your heart, the closer you become to the light. The closer you become to the light, the more clearly you can see.

· ·

Once we allow God to light up the dark places of our past, He often uses that very light to uncover *vision*. The closer you become to the light and the more you can see, the more your God-given vision becomes unstuck. This should cause all of us to jump for joy and to walk in confidence with every step we take. The God from whom nothing is concealed *can* and *will* reveal to you what the darkness holds as He shines His light into your life.

* * * * * * * * * * ❋ * * * * * * * * * *

His light dispels the darkness. . . . His light gives you vision. . . . His light gets you unstuck!

* *

I know it may not seem that way right now. You may be smack in the middle of fighting off some darkness, some tough times, some heartache, or even some unstuck past that still needs to be worked out. But dear sister, I am here to tell you that your Father *knows* and *sees* into your darkness and is Lord over it! Not only that, but He wants to give you vision, His vision, and He wants to shed true light into that very darkness. He desires for you to trust Him, to trust His heart and His plan for your life . . . *regardless* of what is going on.

> Now faith is the assurance of things hoped for, the conviction of things not seen. (Heb. 11:1 ESV)

You see, if left to our own devices and our own ways, we can easily stay *stuck* and even get to the point where we think that the darkness *is* the light—darkness becomes so familiar to us that we begin to become afraid of the light. God forbid, but it's true. I remember reading about some men imprisoned for their faith in Christ who were in especially cruel circumstances—they were put in a small prison with no natural light and very little artificial light. They had no way of knowing the passage of time, their meals were never regular or consistent, and they fought to just stay sane. Staying inside such darkness, among other deplorable conditions, for many years caused their skin to become very pale and change texture, and their minds and personalities also changed. Their eyes adapted to see more in the dark and their other senses became heightened as well . . . and even though they had once lived in the sunlight, they became fearful of it when it was talked about, and they started to cling to their familiar surroundings, trying to make it home. When they were released, they were fearful and upon walking outside their eyes burned with the exposure to the sun; it took them a while to stop cowering and acclimate—but then they relished the sunlight and recognized their old quarters as being the dark and dank prison it was instead of home. The same happens with us when we are stuck in darkness. Those lies, those negative thoughts, those dark ideas can become so familiar that we become imprisoned in them and begin to believe the darkness is normal and good; that not having light, or having very little light, is "just the way I am" or even "God's best for me."

Yes, God created the light and the dark, but the Father also sent the Son, Jesus, so you and I would live our lives unstuck and no longer be imprisoned by the darkness. I sometimes struggle, even writing these pages, with stuck thinking and pressing in to walk in the light that dispels the darkness. But I have come to the conclusion that trusting the Light of the World, Christ, with my darkness (questions, unknowns, fears, and so forth) illumines my heart and my confidence as I continue to walk and live. The more I embrace God and His unhindered vision for every aspect of *my* life, the more I truly see how much I am loved, provided for, accepted, and worthy in that same sight. The more I trust God's vision, the more I realize I cannot trust what I see with my eyes and with my circumstances. The more I realize I cannot trust in my own perception, the more I learn how to walk close to my Savior, knowing He is very familiar with the path He is leading me on . . . and *nothing* escapes His sight.

I challenge you to trust God's vision in your life: that nothing is hidden from Him, that nothing takes Him by surprise, that He

Light Your World

Stuck women trust their own vision. Unstuck women trust God's vision.
Stuck women try to light their own way. Unstuck women let God light their way.
Stuck women accept the darkness. Unstuck women let God dispel it with His light.

So let the Light of God's Word illumine your heart and then hold tightly to God's vision for your life.

loves you and sees the entirety of exactly where you are, right now, in the midst of your circumstances.

> Trust in the LORD with all your heart
>   and lean not on your own understanding;
> in all your ways submit to him,
>   and he will make your paths straight. (Prov. 3:5–6)

Section Three

Purpose
in the Present

Psalm 139:13–18

For you created my inmost being;
    you knit me together in my mother's womb.
I praise you because I am fearfully and wonderfully
    made;
    your works are wonderful,
    I know that full well.
My frame was not hidden from you
    when I was made in the secret place,
    when I was woven together in the depths of the
      earth.

Your eyes saw my unformed body;
    all the days ordained for me were written in your
      book
    before one of them came to be.
How precious to me are your thoughts, God!
    How vast is the sum of them!
Were I to count them,
    they would outnumber the grains of sand—
    when I awake, I am still with you.

13

UNSTUCK
Purpose

For you created my inmost being; you knit me together in
my mother's womb.

Psalm 139:13

Pine Straw Stages

My Saturday morning ritual as a little girl was getting up early,
before my sisters, and designing my version of a pine straw theater
and "stage" in our front yard, complete with ticket booth. Creating cushy seats out of boat safety cushions and a microphone out
of the tallest stick I could find topped with a ball of tree moss, I
would notify my sisters of the impending "show" once they were
awake and bribe them to come. Sooner or later (usually later),
they would begin to gather with their little friends and sit on the
cushions for my "show." I would then begin to mesmerize them
with my "preaching and speaking," usually about why reading was

important or the virtue of not using your older sister's personal stuff. I loved "performing" for my little sisters, but little did I know all those years ago that God was preparing me for my big-girl purpose. I, likewise, didn't know how much this one verse from Psalm 139 would impact my life, leaving me wondering if I would ever be the same after I first read it.

> You made all the delicate, inner parts of my body
> and knit me together in my mother's womb.
> (Ps. 139:13 NLT)

Free to Be God's Favorite

With three younger sisters, this "oldest" often got the short end of the stick. And even though I was *not* the easiest daughter to raise, I longed to be the "favorite" child, but that spot was reserved for my baby sister. Sure, I was a butterfly with a bumblebee sting—bossy and independent, doing everything "my way" as early as I can remember. I don't blame anyone for my bad choices or consequences, not anymore, but I think all little girls desire to be favored.

As God healed my past and designed my future into my present, I have learned to positively capture the way God created me to be. Little do we realize as children that God, in His majestic awesomeness, was thinking of no one else as He knit you and me together in the secrecy of our mothers' wombs. Not even our mothers knew what we would be like before we were born, but God did.

This verse clearly articulates, no matter how you read it, that you and *only you* were on God's mind as He knit you together. We will see, as we focus our life unstuck on purpose in the present, that although God had the whole world in mind as He captured the *purpose* of your life, He only had you in mind as He touched and crafted you cell by cell, organ by organ, design by design, plan by plan.

The King James Version says, "For thou hast possessed my reins" for the first part of Psalm 139:13. Now, if that isn't different enough for you, the Hebrew word for *reins* actually denotes the kidneys. Sometimes when I read God's Word, I want to shake my head and go, "So, God, what you are telling me is that you possess my kidneys?" Almost makes you want to laugh a bit too, huh? Well, God chuckles with me as I dig deeper into His Word, because He knows me all too well. In fact, He knows you too, and your kidneys as well. So, what do kidneys and reins have to do with our "inmost being"? First of all, we need to look at both translations to explain the fullness of just what the first half of this verse says to you and me.

God carefully crafted and owns our inmost being.

In ancient Hebrew times, the kidneys were known as the birthplace of man's (or woman's) desires and longings and were seen as containing the most hidden and vital portion of the human body. That fact brings so much clarity to this verse. God's Word says that God created and possesses our desires and longings—every deeply hidden thing that makes up the most important part of us. Wow! I stand in awe of that. The first time I was confronted with this truth, it really made me see God in a more interactive and intimate way than ever before. Many times I have struggled with knowing that my "heart is deceitful above all things," like it says in Jeremiah 17:9, so I didn't think it was a place God would ever like or claim as His own. But then I came upon this verse and it changed my thoughts, my heart, and my *life*. God created my desires and longings? God possesses my dreams and aspirations?

Yes, ma'am, He certainly does. Why? Because we were created by God for His purpose and pleasure. What an amazing truth!

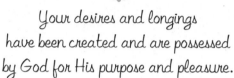

Your desires and longings have been created and are possessed by God for His purpose and pleasure. You are who God made you to be!

> For it is God who works in you, both to will and to work for his good pleasure. (Phil. 2:13 ESV)

But we can't stop here! In the second half of Psalm 139:13, the King James Version says, "thou hast covered me in my mother's womb." So, here we have both the idea of being knit together skillfully and the idea of being covered—both of which are happening in our mother's womb. First, God covered us while we were still being formed, showing His intentional protection of us while we were most vulnerable. Can it get much more awe-inspiring than that? Before we ever knew God or even knew of Him, He protected us as His treasure until He could fully reveal us to the rest of the world. God designed us for intimacy with Him long before we were aware of being alive, before we even had the ability to remember. In the most secret and sacred of places, you and I were under the guardianship and control of the Almighty. He claimed you and me as His own possession and protectively guarded us and continued to form us until we were complete.

> Before I formed you in the womb I knew you,
> before you were born I set you apart;
> I appointed you as a prophet to the nations. (Jer. 1:5)

> For we are God's handiwork, created in Christ Jesus to do good works, which God prepared in advance for us to do. (Eph. 2:10)

I pray that you embrace a sense of divine destiny through these life-giving words, because they shout out the love your Father has for you. Reread those verses. Before you were formed, God knew you. *You* are God's handiwork to do God's works. You were chosen before God even created the world to become adopted into God's family. You see, this proves you are not a mistake or unwanted, that you are loved and God wants your purpose *unstuck*.

Unstuck Truth #13: The purpose of life is a life of purpose!

God designed you with a plan in mind. He is a master craftsman who makes no mistakes, and He wants your purpose unstuck. Not only does this Master know how to create a masterpiece, but no one else can make you better. This Craftsman knows the purpose for His masterpiece, *you*, as well as your immense value to Himself and His kingdom. You have been created well and God calls you "very good" (Gen. 1:31). God also knew the unstuck purpose He intended you to fulfill as He made you in your mother's womb. These plans, according to Jeremiah 29:11, are for wholeness, for your prosperity and not evil, for a hope and a future. You are a one-of-a-kind unique creation and have been intricately designed right down to the number of hairs on your head . . . literally. You are a highly prized possession of the Most High God who loves to show you off. So stop thinking you are a random smorgasbord of attributes that accumulate into something just OK. You are not "just OK." All of God's handiwork, including you, has been declared as very good and *beautiful*. So rest in the assurance that every part of you was forethought and chosen based upon God's purpose for your life. Your purpose is unique and very important to God's kingdom and no one else can do it. No one.

What Is My Purpose and How Do I Find It?

Although we each have a unique purpose, more often than not our unique purpose is uncovered as we step into one or more of five common purposes.

1. God has a fellowship purpose for you.

God started humankind as a team. Remember, He created Adam then quickly saw Adam needed a helpmate. We have been created and designed for fellowship, friendship, and community. You will not experience your full purpose in God alone. Remember my story back in chapter 3 as I shared how much the butterfly in me needed that hummingbird in my husband and the ladybug in my best friend to get started in my ministry? You are the same way; you need other believers who will pray with you, help you see your calling, and share day-to-day life. Have you established yourself in a fellowship of believers? Do you have a church home where you worship, learn, and serve with your gifts? Are you part of a small prayer and accountability group who will pray for God's plans and purposes with you?

> But if we walk in the light, as he is in the light, we have fellowship with one another, and the blood of Jesus, his Son, purifies us from all sin. (1 John 1:7)

2. God has a discipleship purpose for you.

The walk of faith is an ongoing, ever-growing walk. If we are to fulfill our purpose in Christ, we must seek increasing knowledge and understanding of who God is, how He operates, and what His voice sounds like. We have to take time to study what the Scriptures say before we can fully embrace all of God's purposes. God can only use us to the level we desire to be used. We are to be lifelong disciples of God's Word, God's work, and God's will. A mentor of mine told me very early in my walk with Christ, "Pat, you can't give away what you do not have."

> To the Jews who had believed him, Jesus said, "If you hold to my teaching, you are really my disciples." (John 8:31)

3. God has a ministry purpose for you.

I could create a long list here of the troubles in the world. I could list statistics about poverty, divorce, addictions, homelessness, incarcerations, abortion, sex trafficking . . . but honestly, do I really need to? Do you know about these needs in your world, your neighborhood, your family? Yes, of course you do. You know there is ministry to be done right where you are. We do not have to sit and wonder, "What has God called me to do?" God has called you to do *something*. Do what is in front of you. Take the anointing God has placed in you and drop it into the closest place you see needing Him. You may be the only one who says yes to that need today. Be a ministry right where you are, right now, sister. God has called you. He is calling you right now. Say yes.

4. God has a worship purpose for you.

As I write these words to you, my friend, today there is a worship song playing in my home office, telling me to let the weak say they are strong, the poor say they are rich, and the blind say they can see, because of what the Lord has done. Frankly, I couldn't tell you who's who in popular secular music . . . unless I am in the car with my country-music-loving daughter (which is not a bad thing, don't get me wrong). I just normally choose to fill my inner and outer space with songs of praise and worship. I know what I need to keep myself aligned with God's best purpose in me. I choose to have a song of praise rolling in my mind when I wake up in the morning and I listen to it play in my mind all day. When we have worship on our lips it is very tough for the enemy to get anything of his to settle into our hearts. Utter a song of praise today and you will dance in your unstuck purpose of praising your Savior.

> Come, let us bow down in worship,
> let us kneel before the LORD our Maker. (Ps. 95:6)

5. God has an evangelism purpose for you.

My friend, if you have no other understanding of your purpose in Christ, it is undeniable that God has an evangelism purpose for you. This is my proposal. Start with what we shared in chapter 8: your own story. What has been the biggest thing God has done in your life? Saved your marriage? Healed your broken heart? Forgiven a life of past sin? Rescued a child? Walked you through the loss of a child? Healed your body? Held you through affliction? Tell somebody, *today*. There are so many people who need to hear our stories. In the crisis pregnancy center I founded in Tampa we are always desperate for volunteers to come in and share their story and, one day, potentially save a life. Can you think of anything better to do with your day? Your primary purpose is to know God and make Him known!

Stepping into what you know to do, spending time with the Father, and having Him lovingly reveal to you your purpose are the only ways to discover it. You were created to be a unique gift to the world for God's purpose. But all of us have a similar purpose: sharing the love of God with those around us. I love Jack Frost's explanation of this.

> When you begin to experience God's naturally expressed affection and allow it to flow through you to others . . . you [will become] what you were created to be—a gift of God's love to the next person you meet.[1]

144

Remember, sister, you are owned, sought, and planned with a purpose. You are not an accident! God gave you your deepest longings and desires so He can fulfill them. Cease striving, stop working, quit struggling and attempting to perfect yourself, and *rest*. Rest in the knowledge you were made well and are beautiful beyond compare. Relax in the comfort of knowing you indeed have an amazing purpose in this world no one else could fill. Rejoice in your dreams, your longings, your desires—the deepest parts of your soul have been placed by, crafted by, and owned by God. What are those longings that never seem to go away? What are those dreams you have for your life that you so desperately want to come true? Whatever your desires are, the Bible tells us they have been placed within your heart and mind by God Himself for a very particular reason. You have an unstuck purpose! Let's get started on this next section of Psalm 139, knowing beyond a shadow of a doubt that we are a one-of-a-kind unique design and we are owned, sought, and bought for a purpose. Let's pursue that truth together, with the intent and desire of seeking our unstuck purpose.

. . . .

Visit life-unstuck.com for a free PDF, "The Truth about Who You Are!"

14

UNSTUCK

Praise

I praise you because I am fearfully and wonderfully made;
your works are wonderful, I know that full well.

Psalm 139:14

How Is Your Praise Alarm Set?

I remember taking a lazy afternoon walk when my Julianna was just a baby. She was all nestled in her stroller as we headed out just before sunset. We leisurely rambled through a newer, more upscale section of our neighborhood. I was looking at the new houses and silently whining and pining over what I could never have. (Ever been there, done that, girlfriend?) One house particularly caught my eye. It was my dream house: bright white with a tin roof, black shutters, and an amazing wraparound porch. All was quiet; the workers had left the construction site. I pushed Julianna's stroller up the sidewalk to take a peek through the windows. Oh my, what a house. It was everything of my dreams and more. I rolled the stroller around the whole house until I came to the glorious back porch. It was screened in, so I tested the door to see if it was unlocked. I had to see more. Sure enough, it was, so I maneuvered Julianna's stroller onto the back porch. I was just peeking in through the handcrafted glass French doors when all of a sudden a siren went off and a loud voice declared, "Intruder! Intruder! An alarm has engaged! Intruder, intruder!"

Oh my gosh—an intruder? I spun around to see who it was and where they were! Again the loud voice blared. Julianna began screaming and my heart pounded.

"Intruder! Intruder! An alarm has engaged! Intruder, intruder!"

Just as I was about to run for cover from the dark invader, I realized *I am the intruder! The intruder is me!* This amazing house already had a great alarm system installed . . . obviously. It recognized I had stepped onto the porch without being invited, and as I quickly began to escape through the screen door before the police arrived, I realized the door had locked itself behind us. I could not get out! That alarm system not only kept intruders out, it locked them up so they could not escape.

I started freaking out. Then a kind neighbor came to my rescue.

"Don't worry, don't worry," she soothed. "This happens all the time. People just want to peek in the windows and the alarm goes nuts. This is actually my house, so you are fine. We really should disengage the alarm, but we want to keep the building materials safe at night. Here," she offered, "let me take you inside for a closer look."

Wow—talk about good and bad alarm systems.

You may wonder what that silly story has to do with praise. Hang on! Unstuck praise is a lot like my adventure that day. I have learned that praise is a conscious decision and an act of our will. It takes discipline, and often needs to be unlocked and unstuck.

We must keep our internal alarm system armed and ready to ward off any intrusive thoughts that prevent us from glorifying God.

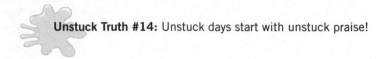

Unstuck Truth #14: Unstuck days start with unstuck praise!

Wonderful Are Your Works, Lord

Clearly the works of God are wonderful, even if we can understand nothing else about them. If you remember, in the previous chapter we touched briefly on how God made us "wonderfully" and "very good," and for His purpose and good pleasure. Now we are going to go even deeper about what an amazing specimen of a woman *you* are, and practice believing it and claiming it as true. We are going to start with the middle of Psalm 139:14, which declares: "[God,] your works are wonderful."

Have you ever thought about God's works, in general? You may have praised Him and stood in awe in His presence as a gorgeous sunset took your breath away. You may have relished the power of the Almighty as you stood on the shore as a ferocious storm approached and waves thunderously crashed. You may have gone snorkeling or scuba diving and seen all the hidden gems God created to swim in the deep. But have you ever paused to think about how amazing the human body and mind are?

Let me share some amazing facts about the human body:

- Heat from our rapidly beating heart would kill us if the heart was not designed with a special lubricated bag that reduces friction.
- Unlike the circuits in a computer, our brain cells are constantly making new connections and "pruning" old ones that are unused.
- You breathe over seventeen thousand times each day.
- Each square inch of human skin contains twenty feet of blood vessels.

148

- You have approximately seventy thousand thoughts per day, although many will be the same ones looping around and around on your pathways.

- You have something in your brain called mirror neurons. If you see somebody stub his or her toe, for example, the same pain area will light up in your own brain, causing you to flinch.

- Humans are the only mammals who have the ability to think about thinking.[1]

Oh my! Those facts are reason enough for unstuck praise. And they are just a tiny fraction of all the amazing aspects of our bodies. Here you are, a wonderfully made human being whose body not only has amazing potential but also is amazing just sitting down. Want to know something else? Our bodies were made to regenerate themselves: our skin sheds itself nearly every month, our liver regenerates, our brain regenerates. With everything making itself new every few months or so, there are still echoes of Eden in our bodies that point us back to the Garden, and how we read we were never meant to die. Is this not awesome? Are *you* not awesome?

Keep Your Praise Engaged

I have an article I clipped from a newspaper during one of my travels that shares a recent study at the University of Pennsylvania called "The Paradox of Declining Female Happiness."[2] The study points out how women in America are less satisfied with their lives today than thirty years ago. The findings were consistent across racial, economic, and age groups. The study was fascinating when you consider how much women's lives have improved over the past three decades. We are better educated, have advanced leaps and bounds in available career opportunities and professions, live longer than ever, and even have men doing more housework. So what was the key reason for this decline, according to the study? Our expectations of happiness have risen, and the world has not been able to deliver!

Now that we have "accomplished" the liberation that we (I) fought so hard to achieve, we continue to need more and more to satisfy ourselves. For our mothers, success was a well-kept home, a successful marriage, and well-behaved kids. Women today expect that *along with* equal pay, equal rights, and a stake in the ground of society. We want all the stuff our Facebook friends have and a kitchen like the one on Pinterest. We want a money-making blog, age-defying faces, and gravity-defying abs.

Unstuck praise requires us to focus on keeping our heart alarm engaged against intruders, and when we catch one, lock them up.

You know what they look like, those pesky praise intruders:

Disapproval and disrespect

Complaints and criticism

Impatience and whining

Disregard and failure to appreciate

Pessimism, bitterness, and discouragement

Do not allow these thieves to steal your life unstuck.

In Psalm 139:14 we are reminded that God *alone* is all we need and praise is the way to life unstuck. The recipe for a good life is not about the car we drive or the job we win; it's not about the amount of money we have in the bank or the size of our home. Unstuck praise and an attitude of gratitude are the recipe for a good life.

Set Your Unstuck Praise Alarm on God

Stuck Praise

I hate my thighs. They were always way too big for my lower legs. My eyes kind of get lost on my face. I have never had great eyelashes.

150

I have always wanted to be more eloquent, to be a great speaker and writer, but other speakers and writers have far better ideas and say cooler things. I am so basic and have nothing great to share, so why bother?

I am clumsy in one-on-one conversation with someone I don't know very well. I can't seem to say the right thing.

I am way too old to accomplish my dreams now. I should have started a long time ago.

Unstuck Praise

I am so grateful for my legs. I can walk, run, and dance.

Thank You, God, for my eyesight. With my eyes I see the hurting, read Your promises, and see You.

Thank You, God, for my love of words. Thank You for opening doors and opportunities according to Your perfect timing.

Thank You, God, for giving me growth opportunities. Help me see each person as You see them so that I can focus on what they need and how I can be a blessing to them.

Thank You, God, that You have ordained every day of my life, and every one was needed for the assignment You have for me. Help me start today moving toward my calling and dreams.

I love the words of Psalm 103 that tell me how to instruct my stuck self and make my heart line up with God's heart. The words say, "Praise the LORD, my soul [my insides]; all my inmost being, praise his holy name. Praise the LORD, my soul, and forget not all his benefits" (vv. 1–2). As the psalm continues, we discover God

forgives all your sin,
heals all your diseases,
redeems your life from the pit,
crowns you with love and compassion,

satisfies your desires with good things,

and (if that's not enough for you, here is the best one) renews
your youth.

Praise has the power to keep you stuck or unstuck right now,
today. So get your praise unstuck, my friend. Let it heal you, lead
you, and cleanse you. Allow God's Word to speak to you and enliven
your weary spirit. Ask God to reveal just how unique and precious
you are to Him and His kingdom. Such knowledge and favor are
too great for us, but He gives them to us anyway. And what is the
result of all this knowledge? *Unstuck praise*. When confronted
with the awesome nature of God—His intimate knowledge of us,
His children; His desire for a cherished relationship with us; His
purpose for each and every person on this planet; His provision
for our reconciliation to Him—it always results in praise. We can
do nothing less when we are met face-to-face with this wonderful
and loving God and are aware of how cherished but broken we are
without Him.

The Gift of Praise

My husband and I can barely step through the doors of our church
these days before someone is stopping us to tell us how "awesome"
and "amazing" our two oldest grandsons are. As teenage boys, they
have both found their age-appropriate areas of service within our
church where they are using their *humongous* gifts and talents. Both
are brilliant technical (sound, lighting, technology) "engineers"
and have inherited their dad's skill for fixing, creating, and building along with their mom's design and crafting gifts. That is all
well and good; we are very proud of their musical talents and their
servant hearts. But more than that, we are bursting proud of AJ
and Jacob for their manners and their honor of adults and those

in authority. Sadly, that is such a rare thing to find in teenagers that people *find us* to praise them for it.

Praise is a gift.

For us to take time and intentionally share the gift of praise with someone else blesses and honors God above all things.

The Bible says:

> Shout for joy to the LORD, all the earth. (Ps. 100:1)

> Sing to the LORD with grateful praise;
>   make music to our God on the harp. (147:7)

> But I, with shouts of grateful praise,
>   will sacrifice to you.
> What I have vowed I will make good.
>   I will say, "Salvation comes from the LORD." (Jon. 2:9)

Life unstuck thrives on praise. Praise God for His goodness and worthiness, and praise Him for others—because He loves that.

So, praise Him and praise His wonderful works, which your soul does truly know. Tell God how thankful you are that you have the ability to even think about Him. Shout out a hallelujah to the Lord that you have been carefully and purposefully constructed. Sing praises to His name that He calls you His own and delights over what He has made. Thank your Father that He makes no mistakes or accidents, especially when He made you—*you.*

. . . .

Visit life-unstuck.com to join our "24 Days of Unstuck Praise Challenge" and be entered to win some free praise reminders!

15

UNSTUCK
Performance

My frame was not hidden from you when I was made in
the secret place, when I was woven together in the depths
of the earth.

Psalm 139:15

Queens Don't Slide

I woke up looking at the most amazing ceiling I have ever seen. For
a minute, I forgot where I was. Then it dawned on me as morning
light filtered through the hundred-year-old lace curtains fluttering
over the Louis XV ivory armchair.

I, Pat Layton, am sleeping in the Florida governor's mansion.

Yep. That's what I said. I was waking up in one of the elabo-
rate guest suites in the Florida governor's mansion in Tallahassee.

My friend, the governor's daughter, was just down the hall in her own bedroom. I was there as her guest and had been invited by the governor, at my friend's suggestion, to be part of a state initiative for the advancement of adoption of children in Florida's foster care system. Lots of people were there, but I was the only one who was sleeping in the governor's mansion. It all felt like a dream and I often had to pinch myself to see if this was real: eating in the governor's private dining room with the family, having tea with the governor and chatting about state child welfare policies, riding in a limo to get to our meetings followed by afternoon snacks with "the press." I was so out of my comfort zone and spent most of the time feeling out of place and insecure. It reminded me of the movie *The Princess Diaries*, where Mia Thermopolis (played by Anne Hathaway) is discovered by her grandmother the queen (played by Julie Andrews).

For whatever reason, I love that scene where Mia instructs the queen to "slide" into her ratty convertible and is immediately informed by her prim and proper grandmother, "Excuse me? Queens *don't* slide."

Mia worked really hard to be not just any high school senior but rather a princess in disguise. I found myself trying to "act" like my friend who really *was* the governor's daughter. I tried to act like, even think like, I belonged in the governor's mansion much like Mia tried to act like a princess. In the end, I had to settle on just being *me* and realizing God Himself had placed me in such a time and such a place to be His ambassador. He allowed me, in a divine moment, to share the reason for my passion for the sanctity of human life with a very pro-choice governor who ended up sitting on a couch with me, tears running down his cheeks, as I shared my story—the word of my testimony. Remember, my darling friend, God doesn't care if you slide or don't slide. His assignments only use those outside things for His inside work.

Acting like somebody else gets exhausting!
Let's enjoy being ourselves. It's who God
designed us to be in the first place.

As I looked deeper into David's words in Psalm 139:15, I discovered that in other versions the words "woven together" are interpreted as "curiously wrought." Here is some of what I learned: the Hebrew word *râqam* means "embroidered, to deck with color, to variegate." It means to weave with threads of various colors. With us, the idea of embroidering is that of working various colors into a cloth with a needle. The Hebrew word, however, properly refers to the act of "weaving in" various threads—as in weaving carpets. The reference here is to the various and complicated tissues of the human frame—the tendons, nerves, veins, arteries, muscles—as if they had been woven, or as they appear to be curiously interwoven. No work of tapestry can be compared with this; no art of man could "weave" together such a variety of these tender and delicate fibers and tissues that go into creating the human frame. Who but God could "make" them? This comparison is an exquisite one, and it will be admired *more* the more a person understands the structure of his or her own frame.

Mia Thermopolis finally gave in to being queen, but she was her own kind of queen.

God says you are His princess daughter. He adores you *now*— just like you are, wherever you are, whatever you are doing. We are not perfect and never will be. We need God's grace, and that is exactly what He is best at giving.

> But you are a chosen people, a royal priesthood, a holy nation, God's special possession, that you may declare the praises of

him who called you out of darkness into his wonderful light.
(1 Pet. 2:9)

Perfect Imperfection

We all struggle with things about ourselves, both inside and out, where we may be a little less confident than others, but do any of those "imperfections" truly detract from our immense value to our Creator?

No!

I have said it before, and it is true—I love social media. It allows me to connect and stay in touch with people I otherwise would never get to interact with. It allows me opportunities to learn, to be inspired, and to share my own life journey with others, but there are those times when instead of taking the *good* out of the cyber world, I do nothing but sink into my "have not." You know it's true. You lay in your bed at night and see the world through Facebook, Pinterest, and Instagram. You scroll through your "friend" list and see how someone had a romantic dinner date with her husband while your husband is watching TV in his sweatpants. You see the picture of homemade cupcakes sitting next to the cute blue KitchenAid mixer in someone's adorable HGTV-designed kitchen, and look up at your ten-year-old refrigerator and hand mixer with no cupcake batter in sight, and think, *My life is far from a tapestry of many colors . . . it is a train wreck in black and white!*

It's a trap, my friend. Don't fall in.

Unstuck Truth #15: "Her" success is not your failure, and your failure is not her success.

A few chapters ago we discussed our emotions, if you remember. In addition to our emotions, we talked about how we *must* align our thoughts with truth in order to truly experience unstuck performance and be who God created, in fact consciously and delicately embroidered, us to be. Our behaviors are the best indicators of what we truly believe. Let's allow God's Word to be our measure of success, not what others are doing, saying, or cooking. Let's step into who God created us to be, where He created us to be, doing what He created us to do, and let's do it like a queen!

Free to Be Flawed

This is probably one of the most difficult aspects of being a woman, or a Christian for that matter, we will ever encounter: we cannot do *anything* apart from Christ. Yes, I know you may have been told you can do anything you set your mind to; you may have been told that the world is your oyster; you may have been told nothing can stop you—but these are all lies. I'm sorry. The truth of the matter is that you and I are helpless when it comes to changing ourselves, especially when it comes to ruling over our emotions. We depend upon God to transform our "natural" with His "supernatural." When we focus on Christ, His thoughts become our thoughts, as we read in Proverbs 16:3. We may indeed teach our children to become more and more "independent" of us from the moment we begin teaching them to walk, but that is not the way God teaches us. His desire is for us to depend more and more upon Him with every passing day, with each passing breath. For God knows we can do all things *only* through Christ. We can be victorious over our emotions *only* when we abide in the Vine. In and of ourselves we are weak. Sure we can walk, feed ourselves, read, and make plans—but in God's perfect perspective of His children, we are truly helpless. The truth is that we cannot take a single breath without God continuing our life. Our heart gains permission from its Creator before beating even once more. Our brain continues functioning only with the approval of the Lord.

The verse we began this chapter with talks about not being hidden from God while we were being formed, and yet we were hidden and protected from everyone else . . . even our mothers! Even with today's amazing technology and 3-D sonograms, no one knows *exactly* what we are going to look like until we enter the light of day. In fact, even then most of us is still hidden from the world by our skin. If we have surgeries, our surgeons are able to see how we were woven together (our organs, blood vessels, veins, muscles, nerves), but even they aren't able to perceive our personality. No one can really see what truly *makes* us except for the One who made us and from whom nothing is hidden. And it just so happens that when He made you and me, he made us fully dependent upon Him. Why? As D. L. Moody is credited with saying, "the world has yet to see what God will do with a man [or woman] fully consecrated to him."

Second Corinthians 12:9 says that God's power shows up best in our weakness. Let that sink in, friend. You are required to allow your weaknesses to be upped by God's strengths!

Can you grasp the beauty here? It is in our *weaknesses* and *shortcomings* that Christ is glorified and magnified in our lives. Only when we are surrendered to the fact that we can do nothing of ourselves can God manifest His strength in us. The very same strength and power that raised Christ from the dead are living within us and are available to us, but only when we cease striving and trying and struggling to do things on our own. The same goes with our emotions. Only a Savior can re-create, restore, and heal our broken bodies and hearts. Only Jesus can heal our emotions. Only when we surrender to Him do we have the strength available to govern our thoughts and emotions. Only then do we experience true freedom. Only then can we truly run with complete abandon and abundant joy. Only then can we give away something precious instead of dirty rags.

●○●●●

As I am writing this chapter, a song is running through my head that won't let go and it isn't "Jesus Loves Me," it's that old Helen Reddy song, "I Am Woman, Hear Me Roar." I am surely dating myself. It was popular in 1975 (I was just a *baby*). I have no idea if Helen Reddy knew Jesus, but one thing I do know: her words were born out of a heart God created. Whether she used her gifts to glorify Him or not, He alone made her a strong, invincible woman.

You are woman—roar, girl! Live in unstuck imperfection.

Three Facts about Unstuck Imperfection

1. We are all called to special assignments. Find yours!

> It is he who saved us and chose us for his holy work not because we deserved it but because that was his plan long before the world began—to show his love and kindness to us through Christ. (2 Tim. 1:9 TLB)

> For we are God's handiwork, created in Christ Jesus to do good works, which God prepared in advance for us to do. (Eph. 2:10)

2. God calls the unqualified. Move into your calling, just as you are.

> When they arrived, Samuel saw Eliab and thought, "Surely the LORD's anointed stands here before the LORD." But the

LORD said to Samuel, "Do not consider his appearance or his height, for I have rejected him. The LORD does not look at the things people look at. People look at the outward appearance, but the Lord looks at the heart." (1 Sam. 16:6–7)

3. There is no better time than right now! In the middle of your imperfection, embrace your place.

If you wait for perfect conditions, you will never get anything done. (Eccles. 11:4 TLB)

Do you remember Moses? He had a speech problem. Paul? He never fully recovered from losing his sight on the road to Damascus. Peter constantly struggled with having his foot in his mouth. The Samaritan woman was defined by her litany of lovers. Mary was fussed at by her sister for not helping her. Samson and David had weaknesses with women. Jeremiah was depressed and Job had some downers for friends. Do you see a pattern here? These were all people who had weaknesses but God used them all—*through* their weaknesses. Moses led God's people out of Egypt, Paul reached myriads of Gentiles, Peter's tenacity with the Jews led to thousands being converted, the Samaritan woman led her town to the Savior, Mary was told she chose the "better portion," and Samson and David were great men of God! Jeremiah was used to tell a wayward people of God's broken heart over their sin, and Job heard directly from God of how He has *all* things under His control. In each of these cases, the individual realized their inadequacies for achieving what God wanted of them. Each person was keenly aware of their need for the true freedom only God could give. And each person had to receive that freedom before they could be fully used by the Lord and give away anything in return.

So cease striving to do it yourself. Cease striving to give away what you don't have. Cease striving altogether! Know that He is God, and freedom and life unstuck are available to you as you surrender . . . sweet surrender. It is there you are made whole; it is there you are made strong; it is there you receive your freedom; it is there you can declare health and wholeness over your emotions and give away that same hope and freedom to others.

. . . .

Join the conversation with other women at life-unstuck.com as we allow God to replace our imperfection with His perfection, and download the free "Performance Fact-Checker."

16

UNSTUCK
Surprises

Your eyes saw my unformed body; all the days ordained for
me were written in your book before one of them came to be.

Psalm 139:16

One Perfect Day

All I could see in front of me was white. Hospital white. White
walls, white ceilings, and bare windows. An emotional battle raged
in my heart and head. My husband, Mike, and I walked the seemingly endless hallway together, just as we had so many years before.
This day we were here to meet our soon-to-be baby daughter. Our
hearts were drawn to meet her. My head was stuck in memories of
another time when we had taken a similar walk, down a different
corridor, in this same hospital. Twelve years before, we'd had an
abortion in this very same hospital. It all seemed so bizarre.

As Mike and I rounded the corner of the NICU into the open nursery area, we trembled, gripping each other's hands. The room was filled with babies, most on chest-high podiums inside clear plastic boxes with two little "portholes" in the front for the doctors and nurses to slip hands through when caring for the babies. Some were naked, with tiny arms and legs flailing wildly with tubes and wires attached to them, monitoring every body function, covered in white sheepskin.

And that is how we first saw her: a tiny baby girl, born to a sixteen-year-old girl at approximately twenty-three weeks' gestation. Her birth weight was a whopping 1.5 pounds and she was ten inches long. Barely the width of a matchbox, she was, without question, the most incredible and beautiful thing I had ever seen. As I looked upon her face for the first time, I was in a trance. It took all I had to not swoon to the floor as I heard the sweet voice of God speak to my heart. *This, Pat, is what I create in a mother's womb. This is why I have called you to do the work I have called you to do.* I felt overwhelming surety that God had literally placed a "pre-born" child in my presence. On that day, I embraced a final word of forgiveness and fresh word of assignment.

As I looked upon our new daughter, Julianna, my mind was reeling—what about "the work" God had "called me to do"? I was very certain He had called me, not many months before, to open Tampa's first crisis pregnancy center, newly named A Woman's Place.

From the moment I had asked Christ into my heart in 1984, He moved into my life in a mighty way. He surrounded me with strong, Christian mentors committed to help me learn as much as I could about His ways. They taught me to love the Word of God and love prayer, and they loved me as the walls of my past crumbled as I set upon a whole new path. The Lord knew how important these friends would be to me as I struggled to believe He could truly forgive a past as sinful as mine. I will never forget the day

He gently revealed the truth about abortion to me. My immediate temptation was to hide and never tell my Christian friends. I was convinced that once they knew the horrible truth, they could not accept me anymore. I was very wrong. Not only did they accept and love me, they became the wind under my wings as they encouraged me into the plans God had for my life. What an awesome God He is, thinking through every detail! On this day, standing amidst the flurry of activity within the NICU, my thoughts swirled over the events of the past few days and how we were standing here today.

My life was a nonstop wave of activity as I ran a full-time insurance agency and parented two sons, a high school senior and a ten-year-old. All the while, I was deeply involved in the preparation of the crisis pregnancy center. It was during this time when my husband, Mike, woke up one morning and announced, "I think we should adopt a baby girl." My response wasn't exactly overflowing with grace when I responded in my "old Pat" way. "Are you crazy? Can't you see how busy my life is? Does it look like I have time for a baby? Besides, we have a senior!" Needless to say, I was shocked and a bit miffed.

We had discussed the possibility of adoption on several occasions. We had two sons and I had longed for a daughter for many years. I always believed in my heart that my aborted child was a girl. It just never happened: too expensive, too much red tape. But time passed, and it was only small talk until that day I told Mike it was impossible. Fortunately with God, *nothing* is impossible. His ways are not our ways!

Mike arrived home from work that same afternoon looking frazzled and pale. He had taken the liberty, as only a man would do, of asking an attorney friend of ours about the possibilities of adopting a child.

"Do you believe in divine intervention?" the friend asked Mike.

"Absolutely . . . why?" Mike asked his friend. The lawyer proceeded to tell Mike he had just hung up from a phone call with the hospital, which had a little baby girl whose birth mother wanted to place her for adoption.

He also knew most people would be skeptical about this adoption because, as he said, "This little girl was born three months early and weighs only one pound. She's likely to have serious lifelong health challenges and will possibly be blind, unable to hear, and disabled. It's difficult to determine and probably will be for a long time. We are not even certain she will live." Mike relayed our morning conversation to our friend, promptly assuring him that though I would probably not be interested, he would talk to me that night.

We sat on our bedside as my husband told me the remarkable story that evening. We were both overwhelmed with emotion, and the next few days proved that this was God's surprising plan for our family.

Our first glance at this one-pound baby girl was love at first sight for both of us. We knew immediately and without a doubt that God delivered Julianna to us. Mike and I spent the next three months going back and forth to the hospital, sometimes twice daily. Each time I saw Julianna, I laid my hands upon her and prayed Psalm 139 and Jeremiah 1 over her. "Julianna, God knit you together in your mother's womb; you are fearfully and wonderfully made. God knows the plans He has for you, Julianna. They are plans for good and not for evil; you will live and not die."

Our friends and family stood with us in faith for complete and perfect health for our baby girl. It was not an effortless or flawless faith. Sometimes I would cry all the way home from the hospital, and ask Mike, "What if she dies?" He gently reminded me of how God pulled this together and, even if she did die, God had planned for us to be her mommy and daddy. She needed us. We became very close to Julianna's doctors and her main nurse, Jayne. As we did, we learned more of her miraculous birth and rescue from death. Not a single NICU team member could deny the miracle of her life or her undefeatable spirit. Mike and I were always aware of what an honor and a privilege we had been given.

Julianna came home with us when she was three months old. She had a head full of blonde hair, perfectly shaped rosy lips, and beautiful pink skin. She was a perfectly healthy four pounds. No complications. No health problems. Nothing missing, nothing broken.

On many occasions I would take Julianna into the pregnancy center with me, and when a young girl would come to the center with abortion on her heart, I would bring Julianna into the counseling room, place her in the young girl's arms, and say, "Precious friend, this is what God knits together in a mother's womb." Many children are alive today because of those moments, but—I almost missed the day ordained for me!

Today Is the Day He Has Made

In all my busyness, in all my preconceived ideas of what God had me doing and how He wanted it done, I almost missed my *today*. We do that, don't we, girls? We allow our today to get stuck. Sometimes we get stuck in the past, stuck in what happened, how things went wrong, or what broke.

Or sometimes we get stuck in the future. We get stuck in what we have to get done, our next assignment, the next bill to be paid, an upcoming school or church event, who is coming to dinner, or even what we need to do before our next vacation. We get stuck in time. However, God's timetable is very different from ours.

> Look carefully then how you walk, not as unwise but as wise, making the best use of the time. (Eph. 5:15–16 ESV)

> You see, at just the right time, when we were still powerless, Christ died for the ungodly. (Rom. 5:6)

In these verses we are presented with two Greek words that both mean *time* but imply very different things. *Kairos* is the word used for *time* in Ephesians 5:16, and means an appointed time, an opportune moment, a God moment. The word *time* used in Romans 5:6 is *chronos* time, and refers to minutes and seconds, like *chronology*. More often than not, we girls are living and thinking in *chronos* time because we are well aware of having twenty-four hours in a day but a hundred hours' worth of stuff to do in it, right? Did you know that in 2012 the average American spent 8.8 hours doing work-related activities, 7.7 hours sleeping, 2.6 hours on leisure and sports, 1.0 hours doing household activities, 1.1 hours eating and drinking, 1.2 hours caring for others, and 1.6 hours on "other" activities *a day*?[1] We can spend every waking moment stuck in *chronos* and completely miss the opportunity to experience unstuck moments found in *kairos*—like stunning sunsets, kayaking with dolphins, or caring for a friend in pain.

Unstuck Moments

Instead of looking at our time like a to-do list waiting to be checked off (I'm talking to myself here!), we need to shift our focus to proactively watching and asking God, "Where are you in my day, Lord?" Instead of viewing time as seconds ticking by, realize not every second holds the same *worth*. Pause long enough to allow God's wisdom to lead you and me into *kairos* opportunities: the five minutes I have to share the gospel with an unsaved friend is more valuable than five minutes spent processing my email.

We must change our view of what the best use of our time *really* is. We want to use our minutes and seconds wisely, and unstuck assignments come more often when we are not cramming as much as we can into twenty-four hours. Instead, life unstuck is enjoyed by women who are sensitive to the Holy Spirit's leading and who step into each opportunity. Be on the lookout for God's unexpected blessings and have the courage to leap upon them with your whole heart, for unstuck women seize these opportunities. Unstuck women allow *chronos* to surrender to *kairos* and are fully invested in their todays.

> *All* the days ordained for me were written in [God's] book. (Ps. 139:16, emphasis added)

When we give God our lives, He begins to give us a word, a promise, and a vision in return. He sets in motion things we could never dream of or imagine, but again it takes the faith to *see things the way God sees them.*

God has written *every* page of our journey and we must be careful not to get stuck in a *chronos*-driven life, missing *kairos* moments God has ordained for us. The truth is, as my Julianna day clearly shows, God shows up in the strangest places when we allow Him to move unexpectedly in our days.

Unstuck Truth #16: Unstuck assignments often begin when *chronos* ends and *kairos* begins!

The Power of Unstuck Days

Michael Hyatt, CEO of Thomas Nelson Publishers, asked his blog readers one day, "What does a 'perfect day' look like to you?" He was faced with the fact that "being a good CEO and being busy" did not necessarily allow him to "live." Being inspired to "live well" and invest in the relationships most important to him by creating as many "perfect moments" as possible, Michael wrote,

> [A perfect moment] is an experience with others when time stands still. It is a time full of the present, when the past is left behind and

the future is set aside. It is a special time of focused attention and heightened awareness. Interruptions and distractions are consciously excluded. Cell phones are off. Hearts are wide open. All that matters is this moment—the people I am with and the conversation we are having now.[2]

So, what does a "perfect day" look like to you? Is it a fish fry with the family finished off with some paddleboarding? Is it an amazingly intimate time with God? Is it a date with your wonderful husband or a sunset walk on the beach by yourself? What are the details surrounding your "perfect day"? Sure, we all enjoy a bit of time where it is all about us, and even go to great lengths to create "reasons" to experience beauty, tranquility, and pampering, but for us to be truly unstuck, we must allow God to break into our day and make it His own.

When That Day Is Dark

We all know life isn't always perfect, don't we? Sometimes when God breaks into our day, it doesn't make sense, it throws us for a loop, and we just don't understand what He is doing. It is then that we just have to trust Him, period, when our day gets dark. You know, the days when bad things happen? Oh my, I don't have to explain about that, do I? I am certain you can bring to mind this very moment a heartbreaking story of someone's, maybe your own, unplanned trial or heartbreak that makes you wonder where God is. Why has He allowed this? What good could possibly come from this pain? Regardless of what happens in our *chronos* day, regardless of what happens in our *kairos* day, *God wants us to seek Him every day, in every moment.* God is in the hospital room and the prison cell. God is in the boardroom and the carpool. God is in the courtroom, the school room, and the bedroom. God is in the bar and on the ball field. God never leaves you nor forsakes you.

170

Consider These Unstuck Surprises

Sarah, Abraham's wife, was an old woman with an empty womb. Then she became pregnant with a child of promise.

David was on the run from Saul's armies being tormented and falsely accused. Then Saul's army was dead and David was king.

Esther was a young girl, uncertain of her future. Then she became a queen and went on to rescue a whole nation.

One day the disciples were hiding away in a secret room, filled with fear and uncertainty. The next they were filled with the power of the Holy Spirit and shouted the truth about their risen Savior.

God always has bigger ideas than we do! So give God your empty womb, your tumultuous future, your persecuted family and friends, your fears and uncertainty. Sister, when you live unstuck and *every day* surrender fully to the Lord, God can not only use you mightily but He can transform your life into something strikingly beautiful and breathtaking.

Live unstuck today and plan to be surprised by God!

17

UNSTUCK
Favor

> How precious to me are your thoughts, God! How vast is the sum of them!
>
> Psalm 139:17

You and Me, Baby, We're Stuck Like Glue

Have you heard that song? I have it as the ringtone for when my honey calls me. I always know it's him and I always smile when I hear it. I also have special ringtones for each of my adult children. It is silly the thrill I get just hearing the sound of each one as they call, especially when I haven't chatted with one in a day or two. I love the sound of my children's voices and love, love, love my "Gs." My family is precious to me. I feel like I am always thinking about them.

This verse reminds us of the good, good love of Jesus—how He is always thinking about us and how vast that love of His is.

Vast. Let's think about that cool word for a minute. Vast: of very great extent, size, or proportion; huge; enormous.

Let me take a shot just how huge the concept of *vast* truly is, OK? Take the twenty-six letters of our alphabet, also known as the ISO Latin Alphabet. As you multiply letters, mix them up, and create patterns with these twenty-six symbols, you can get the English language, right? In fact, the Oxford English Dictionary lists around one and a half million English words, although many are no longer used.

That's pretty impressive, but not *vast.*

Using the same alphabet, we can also create words in Italian, Spanish, German, and French. All of their words combined adds up to almost four million words, all stemming from basically the same twenty-six letters. Still impressive, but still not vast. This is vast: the ISO Latin Alphabet is used to write out the words of over one hundred languages worldwide today. Over *one hundred languages* all use the same twenty-six curves, lines, and squiggly symbols as the basis of how they communicate. *Oh my.* That, dear sister, is vast.

The original idea of "vast" is something so big, or such a large number of things, that it seems as though it cannot be counted. The kind of thing that truly boggles the mind . . . like when some people talk about the number of stars and planets in the universe being greater than the number of grains of sand here on earth . . . *wow!* Now, to drive this idea home: the number of thoughts God has toward *you* is vast.

Not only are God's thoughts of you vast, they are precious; they are personal; they are passionate; they are protective. David treasured God's thoughts of him, and they were not only the things that encouraged David but also *defined* him. God's thoughts of you are vast and *vastly good.*

Unstuck Visibility

David knew what it meant to be seen and to feel unseen. In 1 Samuel 16:11, we see little boy David was out tending the sheep when he was called into his assignment. I love to think about how, as Jesse and Samuel pondered over who God wanted as the next king, David was not even in the lineup. David was with the sheep. David was just doing his thing, all alone. Isn't that a great example of how God sees us when no one else does? Even when we aren't thinking we have an assignment, God is thinking about our assignment. Looking at this moment in time with David, what could he have been thinking about? Was he mad at a friend? Was he upset to be the only one working while the others were invited to dinner? Was a lion stalking him that very moment? We have no way of knowing, or any reason to believe, that David was aware God was, in those very moments, thinking about him and his lifetime assignment. I mean, how many of us (including me) have faulty thinking when it comes to God's thoughts about us? How often, my friend, do you wonder if God even sees you? Notices you? Cares about what is going on in your life? Probably more often than not.

Unstuck Favor Deserves Unstuck Faith

I have a sweet young friend who is truly adorable inside and out. She married her high school sweetheart after he had become a young father with another woman. That story had turned south and the young man ended up with custody of his little girl. My young friend was not hindered; she loved them both. She embraced the daughter as her own. The couple went on to have an adorable little boy and built a beautiful family. My friend was an amazing mom, a servant-hearted family member, and an adoring wife—that is, until the day she stopped by her husband's business

174

and found him in a compromising situation with his secretary. She begged and pleaded for him to not sacrifice all they had for a "fling" but he was too stupid (can I say that in a Christian book?) to stay put. He chose the other woman over his wife and children. My sweet friend was devastated and woke up every morning feeling as if her lungs had been deflated and tomorrow would be forever dark. She felt ashamed, rejected, unwanted, and *definitely* unseen by God. Sometimes our heart is so broken we cannot see ourselves as God sees us. We only see inky darkness and no hope for tomorrow.

Sometimes our childhoods fell short of what we needed or wanted. Bad choices or influences led to thinking poorly of ourselves and transferring those thoughts to God—automatically assuming He thinks of us the way we think of ourselves and the way everyone else thinks of us too. Crazy, huh?

Experience may tell us we are unwanted, and then we assume God doesn't want us either. Do you see how we can have difficulties believing that we are precious to God and that He is lovingly thinking of us all the time?

Unstuck Truth #17: God is thinking about you, fighting for you, chasing you down.

I've seen God answer plenty of prayers in my own life as well as in the lives of many women I have coached over the past years. I've seen family members physically healed, leaving doctors speechless. I've seen God rescue me from crisis. I've seen financial breakthroughs that seemed impossible, both personally and in ministry. I have seen couples labeled infertile give birth to healthy boys and girls. I have seen women facing unplanned pregnancies give birth to miracles. I have held women in my arms as they grieved over choices from the past that left them feeling unforgivable and paralyzed by shame, and I have watched God melt that heartbreak away before my very eyes. It's always awesome when things happen like this, and we see our faith strengthened as our prayers are answered. Praise the Lord! But sometimes—a lot of times, honestly—in spite of our prayers and our pleading for that miracle or that release or that way out, it seems like God turns the other way.

Sometimes I feel like God doesn't see me at all. Sometimes I feel invisible and unheard. Sometimes I pray my best, most honest, most heartfelt prayers—and there is no answer. God does not respond. Or even worse, I know the answer is no. Sometimes the breakthrough doesn't come. The hallelujah *kairos* moment doesn't occur. The cancer grows. The bank takes the house. The marriage dies. The kids choose the wrong path. The friend dies.

Our friend David was seen by God in the middle of the sheep stink and given the assignment, whether he wanted it or not, to be a king. But remember, he had lots of life both before and after that moment, life that was filled with blessings and heartbreak as he walked and lived in his assignment. He killed a bear, a lion, and a giant . . . then he was hunted by King Saul. He was a victorious warrior . . . and then had to hide out in caves to escape Saul again. He had an affair with a beautiful woman . . . then the child conceived in sin died. One of his sons led a disastrous coup against David . . . and another son was known as the wisest man ever. Despite what happened in David's life, he knew God was always thinking vastly good things about him, that God never left him nor forsook him. It is the same with you, sister. God will never leave you nor forsake you. He is always thinking of you, but He never promises life will be all moonbeams and roses.

Are you living in one of those lonely "Where is God?" places right now? Did you think you would have had more goals accomplished by now? Are you kicked to the curb at every turn? Have you lived a good life and followed God to the best of your ability and heartbreak *still* happens and cripples your faith?

These seasons of setback can be fatal to our faith. My friend, we all know it is not in the good times when faith is needed. Faith by its very definition is a strong unshakeable belief in something or someone *without* proof or evidence.

The Bible tells us in Hebrews that faith, God's kind of faith, is all about what we cannot see, and that without it we can't please God.

We can easily slip into a place of giving up, bitterness, or even anger at God when these things happen—or we can choose to convert our times of crisis into the greatest opportunities of our life.

It is in those times when we can't see God that we just have to hold on to our faith, to trust, and to know that God sees us.

Believe me when I say that you cannot number the amount of good thoughts your heavenly Father has toward you! In fact, He cannot *stop* thinking about you and how much He loves you, and He is so proud of you. That is the God we have, *that* is the God who loves us, *that* is the God who wants to give us life unstuck. And it begins by knowing and then believing what *that* God says about us. I am going to ask you, even though you may be right smack in the middle of one of those seasons of heartbreak, to remember what God sees in you and what He says about you.

When you are feeling worthless, you can combat that very thought with verses that contradict those lies the devil is feeding you. You can choose! You have God's strength in you. When you feel as though no one is there who really cares, hold on tightly to the verses that proclaim you are never alone. When the enemy condemns you for your sin, remind him of what God says of your blamelessness and utterly forgiven standing. Did you know God promises to exchange your ashes for beauty; that He is your protection, your rear guard, and He goes before you into battle; that He is your shield, sustainer, finisher, and perfecter? And the list goes on and on. Liberty is realized when these words no longer only encourage us but define us. Then we experience true life unstuck!

We experience unstuck favor and freedom when we think about ourselves as God thinks about us.

You Can Exchange It

We've all said it, right? As you hand over that birthday or Christmas gift that you just aren't sure about to a girlfriend. Or worse, by her expression, you are quite sure she doesn't like the tangerine and lavender scarf you chose.

"You can exchange it if you want to."

We all have that one grandmother or aunt who gives those tacky and memorable sweaters or matching reindeer socks and hat set, right? We just hope she leaves the tags on so we can exchange them for something we will actually wear. Or a well-meaning sister or daughter who got you a gorgeous purse or jacket or necklace, but it was in the wrong size or color? Sometimes we exchange those too. We take something that will not work for us and switch it for something that will work.

This concept should sound familiar by now. Life unstuck is all about *exchanging* what the enemy wants to sell you in lies and deception for what God promises you in truth and love.

God gives us the precious, beautiful gift of choice each and every moment of every day. He urges us to exchange the lies of the enemy for His life-giving identity. It's like making any other exchange in life—for small or large decisions. For instance, I know of a woman who went to the doctor and was diagnosed with an autoimmune disorder. She had some decisions to make concerning her well-being and diet: either deal with bouts of intense pain and take medication along with maintaining her same food choices or *exchange* her current diet for one radically different that would

178

alleviate her symptoms and eventually put her in remission. Another friend of mine was faced with a decision regarding a home: would she stay in her current home in a neighborhood where police sirens and gunshots were often heard or *exchange* her current situation for a different home in a safer neighborhood? You see, we are met with exchanges every day—and each exchange is a choice. Will we exchange a bag of cheesy chips for a salad? Will we exchange watching our favorite television show for playing a board game with the family? Will we exchange a financially secure job for God's calling on our life? Will we exchange the lies and false identity for truth and embody our genuine identity? Only when we decide that our old patterns and thoughts no longer work for us will we want something more, something better.

God is good, at all times and in all ways. God is a good Father to you, and me, and is always thinking about and loving you. He wants to bless your life and He wants you to live unstuck and on purpose.

God Wants You to Live in Unstuck Favor

Do you remember what Jesus said about God the Father?

> Ask and it will be given to you; seek and you will find; knock and the door will be opened to you. For everyone who asks receives; the one who seeks finds; and to the one who knocks, the door will be opened. (Matt. 7:7–8)

Dear sister, you and I both know there are two facts that must both exist in order to receive something: a giver with a gift and a recipient who *receives*. Our heavenly Father is a good Father, and not only can He give us good gifts, He wants to! And I wonder how many of His vast thoughts might just be saying something like, *Oh, I want her to grab hold of the freedom I have for her*, or

I wish she would just look to Me, I have exactly what she wants and needs, or *I love you, I love you, hear me . . . I love you.* But just like anything else in life, we must choose to receive what God is offering to us, His daughters. It is not enough to merely know about the freedom offered to us, or to know about how much He loves us—you and I must receive it with fullness of joy because we know how much we are loved and how many times a day God cannot help but think good things about us, about *you.* Ask! Seek! Knock! Receive!

Believe God's love and *receive* the fact He loves to love you.

Believe God's acceptance and *receive* the fact He loves to accept you.

Believe and *receive* God's truth He declares about you, found in His Word.

Receive the identity He offers you, and exchange your lies for His truth.

Believe, receive, exchange, and change.

Enjoy unstuck favor from the God who is stuck like glue to you.

18

UNSTUCK
Rest

I can't even count them; they outnumber the grains of sand!
And when I wake up, you are still with me!

Psalm 139:18 NLT

Sandcastles and Daydreams

I remember waking up with drool on my chin and lawn chair lines on my cheek. As I stirred myself back to life, the earbuds that were practically melted into my ears clumsily dropped out but I could still hear the same song playing that had lulled me to sleep. A quick glance up and down the powdery white beach of Longboat Key revealed no girlfriend sitting beside me as she had been when I drifted off. The aqua blue waves were darkened a bit by the lowering afternoon sun and the sound of busy seagulls filled the air. I gathered myself together, stretched my arms up and my toes down, then rolled off the beach chair and headed toward the cottage hiding under the Banyan trees behind me.

I could smell food cooking as I approached the rickety screen door and could see my friend happily humming and working in the tiny kitchen. The squeaky door warned her of my intrusion.

"There you are, sleepy head," she said. "I was just about to come after you. Dinner is ready."

My friend had prepared a fresh fried fish, shrimp, and hushpuppy dinner for me along with her world-class chopped salad and a big glass of sweet tea. Oh my, I was overwhelmed. It was precious.

"Why didn't you wake me up to help with dinner?" I asked.

"You needed to rest, Pat! You are wiped out and you cannot keep up this pace," she responded in no uncertain terms. As we sat down to dinner, my friend continued her soft but no-holding-back declaration about my burned-out condition and began to warn me, not for the first time, about how I needed to find time for rest and restoration in order to keep going.

Unstuck Truth #18: God can do what He needs to do through you—without your help!

My life has always been lived in the fast lane. Always. I basically jumped over high school straight into college after dropping out as a junior, getting married, having a baby, and getting divorced all in less than two years. Then I met and married my husband Mike, finished college, had another son, doggy paddled through seven years of marriage madness, jumped into the arms of Jesus at age thirty, and have been living life one hundred miles a minute ever since.

Finding rest and restoration time is a lifelong challenge for me. In fact, I am a bit exhausted right now! I feel like I have been tired for six months. For me to write a chapter on unstuck rest is truly a stretch, but I love being forced into it as I have learned "there ain't no mistakes in God's assignments." Every page of this book comes like a boomerang right back into my own life. This one is no different. This book is my assignment and this chapter is my homework.

As I write this particular chapter, I am less than a week away from my manuscript deadline. It truly isn't like I have procrastinated and waited until the last minute. I have not. This book has been working its way out of my heart for over two years. I stepped into its pages through a woman's conference the Lord planted in my heart three years ago called Imagine Me . . . Set Free. As God has allowed me to offer this conference across the nation, I have both shared and lived this message. I pray you will do the same thing. You see I, like you, have way more than one thing going on in my heart and life at any given moment. I speak at women's events all over the nation and serve on the board of Proverbs 31 Ministries, my local church, and Surrendering the Secret, an international postabortion recovery ministry. I have a husband, three grown children, and five grandbabies. I have a mom who is alive and well, praise Jesus, three married sisters, tons of nieces and nephews, friends, a church, a neighborhood, dirty laundry, and an empty refrigerator.

I'll bet you can relate!

People are always commenting on how "busy" I am, but honestly, I feel like everyone I know is pretty much just as busy. Life is a fast-moving, moment-to-moment whirlwind of passing days. Every "big" birthday seems to get bigger and come faster. I know I am not alone in this; all my friends and family seem to be spinning just as much as me.

Who has time to rest, right?

Wrong. God demands not only that we rest our bodies and our minds but also that we rest our spirits in Him. Life unstuck requires a balance of assignments and rest.

Let me say that another way: life unstuck demands unstuck rest. Never mind . . . that was the same wording. Rest is the balance that comes between life now and life that is to come. It serves as a guard against a life that has gone crazy and a life that is crazy full.

We Serve Best from Our Reserve

A sweet friend gave one of my favorite devotional books to me after a season of speaking engagements where she traveled with me and watched me at work. My friends are always trying to help me get better at this. Bless their hearts! The book is called *The Deep Place Where Nobody Goes* by Jill Briscoe. Oh my. Her words give me a spiritual message every time I read them. Try this on:

> I ran into the deep place where nobody goes and found Him waiting there.
> "Where have you been?" He asked me.
> "I've been in the shallow places where everyone lives," I replied. I knew. He knew.
> He just wanted me to admit I'd been too busy being busy.
> "I'm running out . . . " I began.
> "Of course," He said. "I haven't seen you in a while."
> He sat down on the steps of my soul in the Deep Place, where nobody goes, and smiled at me. Angels sang; a shaft of light chased away the shadows and brightened my daily day. I smiled back.
> "I'm such a fool . . . "
> "Shhh," He said, putting His fingers on my lips. He touched my hurried heart. Startled, it took a deep breath and skidded to a near stop. My spirit nestled in His nearness in the Deep Place where nobody goes.[1]

Oh, how I love those words! In fact the pages of this little book are dog-eared and tearstained.

God is looking for women who will slow down enough to hear Him when He speaks, who are quiet enough to discern when God redirects their course or when He whispers a name in their ear. In order for us to hear God, our hearts must be paused and undisturbed. God wants us to rest in Him and allow Him to restore and revive us for His great work.

Sometimes our "rest" is not simply stopping physical activity. It is not just "getting away." Sometimes, less often but sometimes, this God kind of rest is in the midst of what we are doing and where we are going.

In Exodus 33:14, God says, "My Presence will go with you, and I will give you rest."

Rest is exchanging our frenzy and frustrations, our hurry ups and anxiety for His unruffled peace and His strength. God wants to show how His "thoughts of you" drop right into the middle of your daily to-do list. God's rest and restoration leave us with a divine sense of destiny and the knowledge that God is up to something in our life.

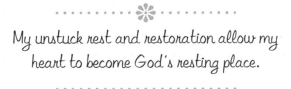

My unstuck rest and restoration allow my heart to become God's resting place.

God is looking for women who slow down long enough to hear and obey when He speaks. Remember what my mentor shared: you can't give away what you do not have.

I hope you will claim those words as your own like I have. You can't spread peace if you are frazzled. You can't bring hope if you are hopeless. You can't share life unstuck if you are stuck! God longs to reveal His holy desires in our lives in order to overflow into the lives of others, but He requires an undisturbed heart. We talked in the last chapter about those times in life when it seems God doesn't see us and doesn't care what is going on in our lives today. I want to remind you, friend—and me too—it is those times when we have allowed rest and restoration to prepare us that make us able to draw upon what God has deposited for the tougher times.

We must exchange not only our thoughts but our frenzy, frustration, busyness, anxiety, and "world on our shoulders" mentality to allow God to be *God* and show Himself strong in spite of our weaknesses, pressures, and circumstances.

God wants to show us what He can do in us and through us—*without* us! Christ's rest comes with the realization that His completed work on the cross has provided all that needs to be done *for all time*. His victory provides life unstuck when we embrace the truth that all the work has already been done to allow us to enter His unstuck rest, His unstuck victory, and His unstuck grace.

In the Old Testament, one of the Hebrew words for rest is *nuah*. It means absence of activity or movement, being settled in a particular place with finality, victory, security, and salvation. The Greek word for *rest* means to cease, refresh, and have intermission.

Take Hold of Rest

One of the greatest joys in our life is to spend time with our adult kids and grandchildren, of which Mike and I have five, starting with our two amazing firstborn grandsons AJ and Jacob all the way to the little ones Mikala, Kai, and Bella. Our too-few times of drawing everyone together under one roof or one stretch of sky always lead to blessings and adventure. I remember one family beach day when our son Andy was entertaining all the kids by feeding the seagulls. Every mom knows it's a no-no to feed the seagulls. Once you start, you can't get rid of them. They literally begin to dive-bomb your head for more of whatever they think you have. These birds got so close to Andy that day that he reached his hand up to grab at one, and much to his shock and surprise *he caught it* by the leg. I don't know who was more shocked, Andy or that bird, but the kids sure were thrilled.

God has the keys to perfect rest, but we have to stop striving and working and rushing and wearing ourselves out before we get a glimpse of that kind of rest. We have to *learn* His kind of rest. We have to grab it! Take hold of it. Don't let it get away.

> Then he taught me, and he said to me,
> "Take hold of my words with all your heart;
> keep my commands, and you will live." (Prov. 4:4)

It's Your Call

If you are living in a season of fast-paced and never finished "overload," God may be calling you to some unstuck rest and restoration. Take some time to seek God and ask Him to help you clear your schedule and set apart some intentional time with Him. The clock is running; make the most of today.

To realize the value of *one year*, ask a student who failed a grade. To realize the value of *one month*, ask a mother who gave birth to a premature baby (or a late baby, for that matter). To realize the value of *one week*, ask the publisher of a newspaper. To realize the value of *one hour*, ask the lovers who are waiting to meet. To realize the value of *one minute*, ask the person who just avoided an accident. To realize the value of *one millisecond*, ask the swimmer who just won a silver medal in the Olympics.

Treasure every moment, friend. Remember, time waits for no one.

Yesterday is history. Tomorrow is a mystery. And as the saying goes, today is a gift; that's why it is called the present.

Simple ABC Steps to Unstuck Rest and Restoration

1. ATTITUDE: admit you are on overload.

God created us capable of disciplining and managing ourselves and understanding our limitations. God also gave us the ability to assess our current situation and honestly discern if we are living overloaded. Admitting you are "overloaded" is the first step to getting unstuck.

I love the story of Joseph and how he instructed Pharaoh's management of the harvest during the good years of abundance (Gen. 41:35–36). He instructed Pharaoh to "store up" grain to be used later when famine would come. It's not so different for us. We have to prepare ourselves through rest and restoration for the assignments (the *kairos* moments) and demands that may be on the horizon. Having a reserve means we don't have to drain our current resources. And when the need comes, we will be ready to say yes to God.

2. BREAK the lie of blame—the real problem is you.

Matthew 11:28 says, "Come to me all you who are weary and burdened, and I will give you rest." Jesus doesn't say, "When I see you get tired and burned out, I will 'beam you up' for some rest." He says you make the choice and *come*. Jesus says, "My burden is light" (v. 30). Therefore, if your burden is heavy, it is not from Jesus. Many times this happens as women, like you and I, continually say yes until we have collected a variety of burdens. We find it difficult to say no and feel it is almost our "duty" to take on one more thing, whether it is through guilt, necessity, or habit. We must exchange our heavy burdens for His light one. Stop the lie that tells you, and me, that we *have* to do something or it will *never* get done . . . or the one that says you can do it yourself. All lies. We were never meant to do things alone and we were never created to walk our

Christian journey alone, either. My friend Lysa TerKeurst says it this way in her new book *The Best Yes*: "A woman is never so fulfilled as when she chooses to underwhelm her schedule so she can let God overwhelm her soul."[2]

3. Schedule CALENDAR times for rest and restoration and connect with God.

Sometimes, as busy women, we need to make the conscious decision to carve out time in our calendars specifically for recharging our batteries. I have a week marked off on my calendar right now in front of me! One CEO I know takes a day or two of vacation before going into her semiannual "deep dives" with her direct reports. She does this because she knows that week of meetings is very draining on her physically, mentally, emotionally, and spiritually. She has a few close friends pray for her during that week for strength and last-minute "help" moments, and then she takes a few *more* days off after these "deep dives" are done to recharge with her husband and children. How are you any different, sister? You may not be a CEO of a billion-dollar company, but your life is no less full of doing "deep dives" with children, teachers, friends, ministries, marriage matters, meal prep, you name it! So, in order to recharge, take time out of your calendar (and stick to it) to focus on the Lord pouring into you so you no longer have to run on empty.

Look at your life, critically. Are you in need of some rest, restoration, relaxation, or reserves? Life unstuck requires unstuck rest!

. . . .

Visit life-unstuck.com for a free download, "10 Practical Ways to Boost Your Energy Level by Doing Nothing," plus a very special downloadable devotional tool to inspire your heart as God's resting place.

Section Four

Passion for the Future

Psalm 139:19–24

If only you, God, would slay the wicked!
    Away from me, you who are bloodthirsty!
They speak of you with evil intent;
    your adversaries misuse your name.
Do I not hate those who hate you, LORD,
    and abhor those who are in rebellion against you?
I have nothing but hatred for them;
    I count them my enemies.
Search me, God, and know my heart;
    test me and know my anxious thoughts.
See if there is any offensive way in me,
    and lead me in the way everlasting.

19

UNSTUCK
Passion

If only you, God, would slay the wicked! Away from me, you
who are bloodthirsty!

Psalm 139:19

Wow! I hear some passion in those words, don't
you? *Passion* is truly an interesting word. During
this writing process I have turned it inside out and
every which way but loose. I have read every verse of Scripture it
is found in and more dictionary definitions than is reasonable for
a brain like mine. So let's talk about passion, shall we?

First, let me ask you: Do you consider yourself a passionate
person?

I consider myself a woman of passion. I have not always known
how to direct my passion, but as I have come to know more about
God, I have come to realize God created me the way I am. He

wants to use my passion for His kingdom purposes. He wants to use your passion as well.

God wants to use your unstuck passion.

David, the author of Psalm 139, was a man of passion. We first see David's calling, anointing, and passion come to life beginning in 1 Samuel, leading us to the epic story of David taking down Goliath.

I encourage you to take some time to review that story, but for now I want to remind you of these words of passion from David:

> David said to Saul, "Let no one lose heart on account of this Philistine; your servant will go and fight him." (1 Sam. 17:32)

David was not afraid of passion. He didn't always express it perfectly, but David expressed passion! The thing is, sister, you and I are not so different from David. There are battles raging in our world, our community, our church, and our family. God is looking for women with passion who will step up and say, "I will fight!" God wants unstuck women who will stand up to the enemy and say,

Get away from me, Satan!
Get away from my marriage.
Get away from my kids.
Get away from my church.
Get away from my ministry.

Are you that woman? My guess is yes, you are.

At the same time, passion can be scary. Passion can be troublesome. Passion can lead to death. We have seen passion do some nasty damage. We all know that passion can be good and passion can be bad. Let's look deeper here and make sure we truly under-stand passion from a life unstuck perspective. Passion by definition simply means "a strong feeling." The feeling can be good, such as enthusiasm or joy. Or it can be the opposite, such as anger or disgust. One kind of passion leads us into unstuck and one leads us smack into *stuck*.

Stuck Passion

In my studies, I discovered that the Hebrew word for *passion* is *charah*. This word is used ninety times in the Old Testament, and many of those times it is used to describe God's feelings of pas-sionate anger against the enemies of Israel. Obviously in these cases God's *charah* passion describes the kind of righteous, pas-sionate anger we talked about earlier, anger that is in response to wrong choices. Outside of God's holy *charah*, this kind of passion is dangerous in almost every other biblical context. It was used to describe anger against someone or their actions. This type of passion could be categorized as *worldly* or *carnal* passion. And both you and I know what happens when we get involved with that type of passion, right? Our mouths get us in trouble, we make rash decisions, and we end up apologizing or wallowing in shame, all because of being led by that doggone passion. Don't feel bad; we have all been there.

Charah passion drove me to defend abortion in my college years. *Charah* was the type of passion that from time to time led King David. Need we be reminded of how David was taken with Bathsheba's beauty and in a *passionate* moment, slept with her and had her husband killed? We have already talked about what happens when we are led by our *feelings*, remember? Nothing good—because those nasty feelings can lead us into lies, directly contradicting Scripture.

195

Charah passion most often leads us girls into unchecked emotions, fueled by our imaginations and fleshly desires, which lead us to dangerous decisions and reckless behaviors. For example, a woman I know was in a heated debate with her tween daughter. The daughter was asking over and over again to go to a friend's house for a sleepover and the mom said no, also over and over. Voices got louder, tones became angrier, and passion for her authority to be obeyed overtook this mamma and she slapped her daughter in the face, as hard as she could, and left an angry red handprint over the girl's eyes, nose, and mouth. Passion got out of control, here. Another woman I know was informed by her then-husband that he'd filed for divorce and she confronted him far from earshot of the children, but her passion got out of control and she started grabbing whatever things of his she could find in front of her and slamming them on the ground, shattering them into tiny shards— beyond all repair. Passion got out of control here too. More often than not, *charah* passion deals with strong feelings and emotions, which cause us to act and react in rash, dangerous ways and lead us straight to stuck!

On the other hand, not all passion is fueled by anger. Some passion is God planted and God honoring. Let me share with you what else I learned in my word digging.

Unstuck Passion

Another Hebrew word for passion is *qana* (*qinah* in verb form) and is translated as a positive form of passion also defined as *zeal*. I love the word *zeal*!

When translated in this context, *qana* passion denotes an eagerness *for* something or someone. It is used many times in the Bible to describe God's passion for us, His joy, and His eagerness for truth, for His name, and for His people.

Qana passion is when you are so moved by something or someone that you move *toward* it in response. Do you remember Nehemiah in the Bible? The wall around Jerusalem had been destroyed and he grieved over it but had a great desire to rebuild it—and, long story short, he did. That, my sister, is *qana*. There was a lady named Mary in the Bible who had been so grateful to and loving of Jesus that she poured her entire dowry over His feet. Again, *qana*. Martin Luther was so disgusted at his church's handling of sin and penance that he wrote ninety-five theses based solely on God's Word and nailed them on a church door—demanding a reformation. *Qana*. And what about the countless women who teach Sunday school classes week after week, driven by the calling to tell children about the love of God? What about the women who work tirelessly at their jobs to bring an end to hunger or orphans or girls captured in the sex trade? What about the ladies who quietly cook for their neighbors who are sick or send cards of encouragement for the downtrodden? *Qana* passion . . . it changes you, and it changes me.

There are some things that I am passionate about, and I'll bet you are as well. I am passionate about my marriage. I am passionate about my kids and my grandkids. I am passionate about my ministry and fulfilling my calling. I am determined that the enemy will not have his way in my family or my life. I am passionate enough to fight like David did when challenged by Goliath. I have learned that when I give my passion to Jesus, no giant in hell can come against the size of my God!

So, we are left with a conundrum: How can we differentiate between emotional passion (*charah*) and godly passion (*qana*)? What's the difference between *good* and *bad* passion?

Unstuck passion is from God for God.

Have you ever been here? Have you ever embraced a good passion that could change the course of your life? I have.

As I entered my late twenties, I ran smack into the truth about human heartache that not only had I never understood but had personally promulgated. As a college student, I lived out *charah* passion about a woman's "right to choose." I never dug deep enough to explore the question, "Choose *what*?" My *charah* passion for legalized abortion was contagious and convincing. I rallied tribes of followers with petitions and written articles. Years later I would discover, through my own bleeding and broken heart, that my passion was tragically misplaced. God began to stir in my heart like He did David's in this verse; He took my passionate heart in His hands and began to shape it for His own purposes. He wants to do that with your passion as well.

Shortly after that encounter with God, my eyes were opened to the lie of abortion. I began to see and hear about the heartbreak and devastation caused by its deadly destruction. A new *qana* passion was born in my life and still burns hot in me today as I consider the words of David in this verse and the God-driven passion that propels them.

● ● ● ● ●

We once had a consultant come to visit our ministry in Tampa to evaluate our staff and help us uncover some placement challenges we were dealing with. He administered some sort of high-level personality/gifts test on each member of the team, starting with me. I honestly don't remember too much about that test or the results but there is one thing I will *never* forget and have recalled on many occasions since. After reviewing my test, the consultant announced in a visibly stunned manner that I had rated "off the charts" and in fact the highest score he had *ever* seen in his career in the character trait called "quick start." A "quick start," by definition of this test, was someone who was so passionate and proactive that they were very quick to take action but sometimes had little regard for the results of their decisions. Wow, did that ever nail me! I am the kind of woman who, once I am convinced I am right about something or that God has given me direction to take, I am *on it*.

As I have surrendered my life to Christ, I have had to learn, little by little and "quick start" by "quick start," how to let God take that personality quirk of mine and make it His. I have had to learn *qana* versus *charah*.

It seems as though passionate feelings can either run amok and out of control or they can be contained and used powerfully. What determines which way our feelings will go? *Who* we let guide them.

Unstuck Truth #19: God wants to take your passions and turn them into His passionate pursuits.

Four Keys to Unstuck Passion

Remember the verse at the beginning of the chapter? David is asking God to kill the wicked people. Wow! I have gotten pretty angry at people before but I have never asked God to kill anyone. We might think this is passionate anger in response to something that happened to David, but we would be wrong. You see, David knew quite well of the holiness of God and how much God abhors evil, *especially* evil done to His children! So here, David is acknowledging God's holiness and God's promises to uphold justice. David understands the first key to unstuck passion!

Key #1: Unstuck Perspective

David basically tells bloodthirsty men to flee from his presence. Why? Because, as Charles H. Spurgeon so wonderfully expresses in *The Treasury of David*, "Men who delight in cruelty and war are not fit companions for those who walk with God."[1] David knows the weight of his need for proper companions, ones who are fit to walk with those walking with God. Companions have a way of influencing our decisions. Listening to what our companions say influences what we think, which also affects the decisions we make. So, as one who was known as "having a heart after God," David knew the necessity of being different from the rest. God had set him apart.

Key #2: Unstuck Pause

David knew his need to be incredibly cautious to choose the right thoughts, which lead to right decisions, which lead to right companions, which lead to right choices. Good choices lead to good passion. My sweet friend Lysa TerKeurst says in her latest book, *The Best Yes*, "My imperfections will never override God's promises. God's promises are not dependent on my ability to always choose well but rather on His ability to use well."[2]

Key #3: Unstuck Purpose

We have already talked about having purpose in the present but I want us to be reminded one more time: our passion must be rooted in God's purposes! Sister, you and I have been set apart and we have been apprehended by a loving God—to capture our purpose in God's kingdom. When passion follows purpose, people are changed. What am I talking about? Do you remember when we talked about our personalities? Each and every one of us has been uniquely made by an amazingly creative and skillful God. Do you remember how we talked about how God fully knows and is delighted by our quirks? And how all of this is only amplified and refined as we forgive others, believe truth, and pursue our loving heavenly Father? And, finally, how each one of us has been created with a purpose? Oh my goodness! Since there is a purpose for your life, what emotions does God want you to channel into passionate zeal and action?

Key #4: Unstuck Prayer

Psalm 139 is one sweet prayer. In fact, a stroll through the psalms will take us on a journey of *passion*. David's transparency reveals his passion, both stuck and unstuck. Both *charah* and *qana* are starkly unraveled throughout the psalms as we hear David's confessions before the Lord. Unstuck passion must be rooted and grounded in unstuck prayer.

Friend, I appeal to you, as Paul says in Philippians 3:12, "take hold of that for which Christ Jesus took hold of [you]." Discover, uncover, or recover your passion and your calling.

Who directs your passions? Which passions direct you? Let's release our *charah* passions and let God take care of that. Let's take hold of *qana* passions and get fired up for God! I want us to grab hold of the abundant life Christ promised us, grab hold of our future, and wait to see what God begins to do in our lives. Let's begin to take those steps to unstuck passion and start to soar.

Each time we are presented with an issue that tugs at our hearts and minds, we are given a choice by God either to let Him use it and us for His purpose or to take things into our own hands. Only when we allow the Father to take our out-of-control emotions and fiery feelings can He mold them and shape them into true passion, *qana*, for His kingdom and His purpose.

20

UNSTUCK
Woman Warrior

They speak of you with evil intent; your adversaries misuse
your name.

Psalm 139:20

You, My Friend, Have Been Drafted

America loves fireworks! In the United States we celebrate several
sizzling holidays set aside to commemorate those veterans who
have served or who have lost their lives in service to our country.

My husband, Mike, was, and as far as I'm concerned still is, a
soldier. He gave his country his nineteenth year of life while serving
in Vietnam as a Marine. As a "forward artillery observer," his job
was to move ahead of the troops into enemy territory, and when
he spotted the enemy to call in the artillery. *Oh my.* I have always

loved that story and have always connected Mike's assignment on the battlefield to the life assignment we women have today.

Mike has never talked much about his days in Vietnam; he has just never been able to share many details about what he saw there, but I have gotten enough of his heart to know that my husband was changed forever by his thirteen months on the battlefield. As I was writing this chapter I asked Mike, "What are five words that would describe your time as a Marine?" These are the words he used:

Honor

Courage

Brotherhood

Freedom

Home

"Those are words you would use today," I said. "What words would you have used as a nineteen-year-old boy sitting in a field surrounded by mud, enemy explosions, dead bodies, and injured buddies?" As Mike's facial expression changed, he got that look in his eyes he always gets when he thinks of Vietnam. These are the words Mike used with those memories in his mind:

Sweat

Blood

Pain

Sorrow

Home

Notice the difference. When Mike considered the *value* of his service, he thought of the results of his service. However, when he considered the *investment* of his service and saw himself on the battlefield, he thought of the pain and loss he endured. The truth is, my friend, life unstuck is a battlefield. As a woman today, regardless of your age or current life circumstances, you have much to fight for and lots at risk. Remember these words from the Bible:

> Your adversary the devil walks about like a roaring lion, seeking whom he may devour. Resist him, steadfast in the faith. (1 Pet. 5:8–9 NKJV)

The devil is always—*always*—working against us. He is after whatever you have! He is after your marriage, your family, your friendships, your welfare, your ministry, your witness, your testimony, your freedom, your life unstuck—and he is as sly as a snake about it.

> And no wonder, for Satan himself masquerades as an angel of light. (2 Cor. 11:14)

We have looked quite a bit over the past few chapters at the ways the enemy slides into our lives and leaves us *stuck*—in our thoughts, our words, our past pain, and our mistakes. In this chapter, I want to pretend we are "forward artillery observers." I want us to get on our hands and knees, metaphorically speaking, and take a look at where he might be attacking in our lives right now, today. I want us to practice the offense versus the defense we have shared over the past pages.

I love how "home" was Mike's landing place on both of his lists. As women, home is, as they say, where our heart is. My homework has told me that the average reader of my book will be a married woman between the ages of thirty and sixty. She will be married or divorced and have children from toddlers to grown and married themselves. At the same time, I know from my conferences that I will have a young unmarried cutie or two holding this book as well. I have a daughter who fits that definition so I know she is reading this (thank you, honey) and has passed it on to a few girlfriends (thank you, sweet darlings) so I do not want you to tune out! Please listen up and let's talk about some real tough stuff for a minute.

Unstuck Truth #20: You have a *real* enemy who is *really* out to steal what God has for your life.

That is not spiritual "church talk." It is real. You are in a real battle right now, today, whether you know it or not, whether you have been thinking that way or not, whether you choose to follow God's plan and instructions or not. Trust me, you are at war.

When Mike was laying belly-down in the mud and grasses of Vietnam, he had a choice. He could ignore the training he had received before being sent out on his own and do things his own way, or he could take advantage of what he had been taught, the armor he had been assigned, and the fact that somebody had his back. When Mike slithered to the spot where he actually saw the enemy, he had somebody to call back to for help; somebody who would send the troops his way; somebody who could supply more artillery. Let me remind you, my friend: the enemy is real and he is after you. So what do we do about it? How do we fight him? We do what us girls love to do . . . we choose the right outfit!

> Be prepared. You're up against far more than you can handle on your own. Take all the help you can get, every weapon God has issued, so that when it's all over but the shouting you'll still be on your feet. Truth, righteousness, peace, faith, and salvation are more than words. Learn how to apply them. You'll need them throughout your life. God's Word is an *indispensable* weapon. In the same way, prayer is essential in this ongoing warfare. Pray hard and long. Pray for your brothers and sisters. Keep your eyes open. Keep each other's spirits up so that no one falls behind or drops out. (Eph. 6:13–18 Message)

> For though we walk in the flesh, we are not waging war according to the flesh. For the weapons of our warfare are not of the flesh but have divine power to destroy strongholds. We destroy arguments and every lofty opinion raised against the knowledge of God, and take every thought captive to obey Christ. (2 Cor. 10:3–5 ESV)

Behold, I have given you authority to tread on serpents and scorpions, and over all the power of the enemy, and nothing shall hurt you. (Luke 10:19 ESV)

For everyone who has been born of God overcomes the world. And this is the victory that has overcome the world—our faith. (1 John 5:4 ESV)

Cover Thy Bottom!

No, honey girl, I'm not referring to your short shorts. I'm talking about your battle fatigues.

I have a girlfriend who tells the story of going to the bathroom on an airplane. Just as she was about to sit on the potty she remembered she had forgotten to cover it with paper. As she proceeded to maneuver herself around in that tiny bathroom and grab the paper, she heard a sweet voice behind her say, "Ma'am, I'm just going to close this door for you, OK?"

My friend proceeded to die a thousand deaths as she realized her naked bottom had been pointed out of the airplane bathroom door, right into the aisle. Unlike my own naked bottom story from chapter 1, she was not drugged on "yum-yum" but was fully aware upon exiting the bathroom that she had no secrets in first class!

● ● ● ● ●

I want us to think for a minute about something us girls often find ourselves talking about—fashion! There is something about being with a group of females that often leads to chatter about shoes or purses. Life unstuck is no different and requires a fashion discussion. In this chapter I want to talk very specifically about the dress code for an unstuck woman warrior.

The Bible tells us we do not fight this battle in the same way Mike fought in Vietnam, with actual guns and actual bullets. The

Bible reminds us that the battle we girls fight today is a spiritual battle and is fought on an unseen battlefield, albeit one that is just as real. Spiritual warfare is about fighting, but the weapons we fight with are not the weapons of the world. On the contrary, they have divine power to demolish strongholds.

In Beth Moore's book *Breaking Free*, she defines a *stronghold* as

> anything that exalts itself in our minds, pretending to be bigger or more powerful than our God. It steals our focus and causes us to feel overpowered, controlled or mastered. Whether the stronghold is an addiction, unforgiveness towards a person who hurt us, or despair over a loss, it is something that consumes so much of our emotional and mental energy that abundant life [i.e., life unstuck] is strangled—our callings remain largely unfulfilled and our believing lives are virtually ineffective. Needless to say, these are the enemy's precise goals.[1]

Beth points out that our main battlefield is in the mind, or our thoughts. We talked about that in detail in chapter 2 so let's talk a bit here about the "dress code" God has established for his daughters as we seek to embrace unstuck victory.

Say Yes to the Dress

Believe it or not, God even cares about fashion. I love that. I love clothes. As you could easily see on my "yes clothes" Pinterest board, I have always been a fashionista wannabe. I have always spent a good bit of my extra money on clothes. Now, I'm not that creative or original, but I do like to stay with current colors and fabrics. As I get older, though, I struggle a bit with not wanting to dress too young. Don't get me wrong, I happen to love the younger styles, but my changing body says no to that adorable dress more often than yes. But, I am here to tell you that God truly touches every

The Best Dress Code

Let's take this verse and contemplate it from this dress code perspective. Here is the outfit God wants you to wear every day:

Belt: A belt here is so much more than a method of keeping your pants from falling to the ground. The belt wraps around your waist, just as we are to have God's Word wrapped around us. Spending time with the Lord and memorizing His Word allows God's power to, in essence, be wrapped around you much like a belt wraps around your waist. Scripture calls it "a belt of truth." Without truth, we cannot fight.

Breastplate: OK, so bras are incredibly helpful in keeping the "girls" from being droopy, and if our bra is pretty and lacy it really does give us some confidence in knowing we are wearing something beautiful, even if no one else gets to see it! Well, a breastplate is similar in that it provides confidence to the warrior that her heart and other vital organs are protected. Christ's righteousness, which is given to us when we choose to follow Him and forsake all others, is what protects our hearts and our intentions. Remember, we cannot achieve righteousness on our own. We must be given true righteousness through Christ's atoning work on the cross.

Shoes: I love shoes. I love finding the perfect pair to complete a stunning ensemble, don't you? Warrior shoes take us places. Being ready to share the gospel and the word of our testimony gives us a firm footing on the battleground and keeps us from stumbling and injuring our tender feet.

area of our lives—sex, money, friendships, vacation time, and yes, even clothing.

Finally, be strong in the Lord and in his mighty power. Put on the full armor of God, so that you can take your stand against the

Jacket: Jackets can be the perfect accessory. They can be an amazing statement piece or merely functional, but it is awesome when they can be both. Just like a jacket slung over our forearm, ready to protect us from the elements of rain or snow, the shield of faith is there to protect us from the elemental weapons of the enemy. Faith must be exercised and must be lifted high when the enemy strikes. We do *not* have puny faith . . . faith in Christ and in God's Word is more than enough to hide behind, and can extinguish fiery darts. But we must hold it up and stay behind it!

Hat: When I think of hats, I think of those worn to the Kentucky Derby or the Ascot Races in England. Those are hats! Big, small, ornate, colorful, with or without bows or feathers, but *never* dull. Hats were originally created to keep the sun off our heads and faces but have since become more of a fashion statement. But helmets? They are still needed for protection! Helmets protect our brains, right? But they also protect our eyes, our ears, and our mouths. Salvation is what guards our thoughts, gives us the proper sight, filters in the right sounds, and protects our mouths so we can say uplifting and good and holy words.

Purse: OK, don't get me started on purses! This just might be my weapon of choice. A purse, the tool we hold in our hands, equals a *sword*. Some purses are smaller and more compact, but regardless of the size they can all be wielded as a weapon against an attacker. We have been given one weapon, and only one weapon, when it comes to spiritual warfare—the Sword of the Spirit, also known as the Word of God. Scripture! Remember when Jesus was tempted by Satan in the desert? His weapon of choice was Scripture. We are no different. When the enemy attacks, take out your Sword, your Bible or the Bible you have hidden in your heart, and slash away at the enemy.

devil's schemes. For our struggle is not against flesh and blood, but against the rulers, against the authorities, against the powers of this dark world and against the spiritual forces of evil in the heavenly realms. Therefore *put on the full armor of God*, so that when the day of evil comes, you may be able to stand your ground, and after you have done everything, to stand. Stand firm then, with the *belt* of truth buckled around your waist, with the *breastplate* of righteousness in place, and with *your feet* fitted with the readiness that comes from the gospel of peace. In addition to all this, take up the *shield* of faith, with which you can extinguish all the flaming arrows of the evil one. Take the *helmet* of salvation and the *sword* of the Spirit, which is the word of God. (Eph. 6:10–17, emphasis added)

21

UNSTUCK
Emotions

O Lord, shouldn't I hate those who hate you? Shouldn't I
despise those who oppose you?

Psalm 139:21 NLT

Many years ago, as God led me out of the pain of my
stuck past and I started to see the lies I had been told,
I realized the detached attitude my ob-gyn had when
I asked about abortion. When my eyes opened to what I had done,
I was very angry with myself and with my husband, but I was even
angrier at that doctor. He should have told me the truth. Wasn't
he trained to protect life? Why didn't he tell me the truth about
what a twelve-week-old pre-born baby looks like? What they *feel*?
I was very, very angry.

Then there was the time after opening my pregnancy resource
center I had the grand idea of sharing our services with the executive

director of the local abortion clinic. I thought, *If she only knew of the options for women, she would surely send more women our way. After all, she is for* choice, *right?* Wrong! As I sat with this woman at lunch, sharing about the free services we offer women at the center, she began to "share" her services with me to the point I almost lost my lunch.

This woman, with a straight and determined face, began to tell me how she worked in multiple positions at her clinic "to serve women" and even sometimes was responsible for "counting body parts" to be sure "nothing was left behind." *Wait, did I just hear what I thought I heard? This woman actually counts the arms and legs and body parts of aborted babies?*

I was so far beyond stunned I can't even remember how I responded at the time; God surely gave me the words, but this I do know . . . I can relate to David's question: "God, shouldn't I hate her?"

I'll bet you have a question or two as well—right? Something like,

Should I hate the neighbor who molested my sweet daughter?

Should I hate the thief who stole my car?

Should I hate the boy who got my daughter pregnant?

Should I hate the husband who cheated on me and destroyed our entire family with his lust?

Should I hate the boss who keeps passing me over for the woman with the low-cut blouse?

Have You Ever Hated Anyone?

David is transparent and real in every way, expressing both good passion and bad passion. Remember in verse 19, when David asked God to "destroy" his enemies on his behalf? I totally understand David's question here. Interestingly, it is the first time in these twenty-four verses where David asks God a question. Every other line of this song has been a statement of David's opinion or perspective, but here David poses a question. I can almost hear him passionately begging for permission, can't you?

God, should I hate them?
God, do I have to forgive them?
God, can I keep away from them?

I can relate. I have often wanted to hold on to hate. The answer is no, my friend. God says no.

Unstuck Truth #21: Stuck emotions are like drinking poison and expecting somone else to die.

We have to understand the root meaning of David's words in this verse. David is *angry*. He is passionate about his feelings but he is inquiring of God from that deep place inside that knows the answer, because we know God! Deep underneath David's passionate anger we find the flipside of passion—life unstuck. David knows in his heart, because his heart belongs to God, that in spite of others' ugly sin, hate will only keep him *stuck*.

The choice between stuck and unstuck depends upon David's right to choose who he connects with, who he associates with, who he wants to do life with. But he has no option to choose hate. David has a decision to make, as he considers God's answer in this moment of passion for his future: to keep his current friends or choose friends of different character.

> Blessed is the one
>   who does not walk in step with the wicked
> or stand in the way that sinners take
>   or sit in the company of mockers. (Ps. 1:1)

Unstuck Emotions Equal Unstuck Women

Has anyone ever cheated you in business and gotten away with it? Maybe stolen money from you, or cheated you out of an inheritance? How about this one: Has anyone ever seductively slipped into your marriage and stolen the heart of your husband? Have you ever watched someone you love be ripped from your life—a child? A parent? A friend? Has someone violated your innocence, or worse yet, that of your child?

Are you familiar with that feeling that sits in a tiny sliver of your heart and mind and leaves you constantly straddled between breaking down into tears and rising up into outright "Let me at 'em!" rage? I think we all have. There are things that happen in this life, no matter how much we love Jesus and have a heart after Him, that can, when allowed to, create a rage that can grow within us like the roar of an ocean fueled and fed by a hurricane. Hate is fed by passion. Passion trapped within hate, anger, and unforgiveness can eat you from the inside out. Passion captured by Christ can change the world.

Our Emotions: the Good, Bad, and Ugly

Anger, fear, and determination are very powerful emotions, wouldn't you agree? Although most of the time they are viewed as negative emotions that should be controlled, God created our emotions—including anger—for our benefit. However, when we don't use emotions properly, we can do a lot of damage to ourselves and to others.

The Bible has much to say about how to handle our emotions the right way.

> Laying aside falsehood, speak truth each one of you with his neighbor, for we are members of one another. Be angry, and yet do not sin. (Eph. 4:25–26 NASB)

According to Ephesians 4:26, it is OK to be angry. Unstuck anger is a God-given emotion and is not a sin, but how we *deal* with our anger may be sinful in nature. Anger is dangerous and destructive when we intentionally hurt ourselves and others. If we hold on to our anger for weeks, months, or years, then it can overtake our lives and consume all of who we are: every thought and every action is motivated by anger and results in bitterness. The person God created us to be ends up buried deep beneath our anger, with resentment and bitterness piled up on top.

The words "Be angry" in Ephesians 4:26 are written in the Greek imperative tense used for commands or direct instructions. You mean there are circumstances when God actually *commands* us to be angry? Yup. To help us understand this, there is an example for us in the Bible: Jesus! Good enough?

When Jesus came upon some businessmen who were cheating and extorting people who came to the temple to worship God, He responded with some fiery emotion—He got angry and everybody knew it.

> The entire city of Jerusalem was in an uproar as he entered. "Who is this?" they asked. And the crowds replied, "It's Jesus, the prophet from Nazareth in Galilee." Jesus entered the Temple and began to drive out all the people buying and selling animals for sacrifice. He knocked over the tables of the moneychangers and the chairs of those selling doves. He said to them, "The Scriptures declare, 'My Temple will be called a house of prayer,' but you have turned it into a den of thieves!" (Matt. 21:10–13 NLT)

Jesus knew the power of unstuck emotions. He did not hurt anyone. Yes, there was a mess, but Jesus's anger was a righteous anger. He was angry and frustrated when he saw how the people of Jerusalem were treating the temple: they had turned a holy place into a market, a place where people were taking advantage of others, and a place of business—not of worship. And He responded.

From this story we can see that anger is justified when it is not a means to selfish gain or a way to hurt someone. Unstuck anger is justified when it results in a change and makes the world a better place. Unstuck anger is justified when we look at someone and feel the anger God has, a righteous anger. It's important for all women to express their anger in healthy and constructive ways. Dealing with stuck anger allows us to move into the crucial area of unstuck forgiveness.

Working Emotions Out

When it comes to your emotions, are you an imploder or an exploder? Dr. Gary Chapman describes two unhealthy ways of managing our emotions: holding them in or expressing them with aggressive behaviors.[1] *Implosive* emotion is internalized emotion, such as anger that's never expressed. "I'm not angry, just frustrated," or "I'm not mad, just disappointed" are common expressions of an imploder.

> Be angry, and yet do not sin; do not let the sun go down on your anger, and do not give the devil an opportunity. He who steals must steal no longer; but rather he must labor, performing with his own hands what is good, so that he will have something to share with one who has need. Let no unwholesome word proceed from your mouth, but only such a word as is good for edification according to the need of the moment, so that it will give grace to those who hear. Do not grieve the Holy Spirit of God, by whom you were sealed for the day of redemption. Let all bitterness and wrath and anger and clamor and slander be put away from you, along with all malice. Be kind to one another, tender-hearted, forgiving each other, just as God in Christ also has forgiven you. (Eph. 4:26–32 NASB)

Unexpressed or bottled up emotions give the devil an opportunity to create a *stronghold* in your life, like we talked about in the last chapter, in your life that ends up grieving the Holy Spirit. When we grieve the Holy Spirit, bitterness, wrath, anger, clamor, slander, and malice are given freedom to rule our life. In verse 29, the word *unwholesome* means "rotten." Stuck anger, as with any unhealthy emotion, can lead to rottenness if it is allowed to just fester in your life. It *will* consume all that you do and all that you are—eventually letting shame, fear, bitterness, and unforgiveness define you.

The results of implosive emotions are passive-aggressive behavior, displaced anger, physiological and emotional stress, resentment, bitterness, and hatred. Imploders typically keep score, so the potential for a delayed explosion from a dormant volcano is always possible. When Paul advised, "Do not let the sun go down on your anger," he was telling us to deal with anger promptly and effectively before it can spread and do more damage. He also warned, "Do not give the devil an opportunity." Paul explained that poorly managed anger offers the devil a *topos*—a plot of land in our lives. He uses that *topos* as a military base from which to launch more attacks into our lives and relationships. Implosive anger leaves you stuck.

Explosive anger is the other unhealthy, ungodly management technique. It's characterized by uncontrolled fury that may manifest in verbal and/or physical abuse. According to Ephesians 4:31, the outcome of all poorly managed anger is bitterness, wrath, more anger, clamor, slander, and malice. Explosive anger verbally attacks by screaming, cursing, condemning, name-calling, humiliating, or threatening. It damages self-esteem and trust and ultimately destroys a relationship when the exploder causes their recipient to retreat for emotional safety. Exploders frequently blame their victims for their anger or minimize their outbursts by calling them "blowing off steam" or "getting something off my chest." In extreme cases, the exploder may grab, push, or strike in anger. All unhealthy anger is harmful, but physical abuse should never be tolerated. Explosive anger leaves you stuck.

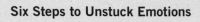

Six Steps to Unstuck Emotions

Ephesians 4:25–32 provides a perfect place to settle the passion of our emotions so we can apply them as power for a passionately unstuck future. Take a look:

1. **Assess your primary emotion.** Does your anger, fear, or resentment stem from loss of control, hurt, or indignation about wrongs?
2. **Take off your mask.** Open up about what hurt you and talk through your feelings with a trusted friend, mentor, or counselor (vv. 25–26).
3. **Deal with issues, and when it is appropriate, confront.** Communicate issues clearly and early. Be sure the goal is resolving issues, not getting back at people (v. 28).
4. **Don't let stuck emotions fester and rot.** Stuck passion is a written invitation to the enemy to exploit us into wounding others and ourselves (v. 29).
5. **Turn to God like David did.** God cares deeply about your feelings. Allow Him to speak to you through His Word and the Holy Spirit. Let God process your passion and turn it into unstuck power. His heart aches when we allow rage, resentment, or bitterness to root (v. 30).
6. **Replace stuck emotions (fear, anger, heartbreak, rebellion) with unstuck emotions (forgiveness, compassion, truth).** Because God has forgiven us so much, we need to be willing to forgive others (v. 32).

Unresolved anger finds many unhealthy ways to express itself.

When one's sense of right is violated, that person will experience anger. He or she will feel wronged and resentful at the person (or persons) who have violated. [Women] often react to things in ways they don't understand. They find themselves overreacting to events and circumstances in ways they don't expect—sometimes

218

with anger, or other times with great sadness or hurt. Now that you are on your healing journey, you can begin to make sense of these uncomfortable emotions.[2]

Let's follow David's example and be transparent about our emotions, and allow God to use them for His glory and our life unstuck.

. . . .

Visit life-unstuck.com for a list of "5 Lies that Keep You from Dreaming!"

22

UNSTUCK
Focus

Yes, I hate them with total hatred, for your enemies are my enemies.

Psalm 139:22 NLT

Nothing to Prove and Only One to Please

The first time I remember being caught in a lie was when I was about eight years old. I was at a cookout with family on the beach when all of a sudden, out of the blue, my younger sister started crying. I had *no* idea what happened. That was the report I gave to my mother, anyway. Little did I know that she had actually watched me drop a fiddler crab into my sister's T-shirt. The crab had mostly just scared my sister but she acted like I was an ax murderer. Needless to say I got into deep water with my mom for lying. And as you can hear in my words, I was the one who was permanently scarred.

Thus is the life of "sisterhood"—both biological and spiritual. No one has to teach us to be competitive, to outdo one another, or to try to appear smarter, superior, or better than the next person. It is our natural bent to compare ourselves with others to see how we "measure up." The bad news is neither the measurer nor the measured are perfect. In this verse of Psalm 139, David is making the big, *huge* mistake of comparing his loyalty and commitment to God with someone else's.

God says, *Don't do that!*

Our wonderful friend David is missing the truth here—God *loves* those dastardly enemies of David's and desires to have them turn around and face Him. God says, *Don't compare yourself with anyone else.*

> For everyone has sinned; we all fall short of God's glorious standard. Yet God freely and graciously declares that we are righteous. He did this through Christ Jesus when he freed us from the penalty for our sins. (Rom. 3:23–24 NLT)

Unstuck Potential

The first thing I see happening with David in this verse, which threatens to get us stuck too, is *misdirected focus*. As we have clearly seen, God has set us apart for very specific purposes for specific seasons of life. I believe our entire life should be *about* that season's purpose. As He did with David, sometimes God reveals our primary purpose early in life and sets our course, steady on. Other times we just keep doing what we are doing until He reveals what He wants to reveal, when He wants to reveal it, and how He wants to reveal it. Life unstuck demands keeping our focus on *exactly* what God is doing in our lives at any given moment, stepping into each day looking for that *kairos* moment, doing what He has placed in our paths that day to the best of our ability. We get stuck when we worry about what somebody else is doing or not doing.

Unstuck Truth #22: Sometimes we have to change our position to change our perspective. Stay focused on your potential, not your problems!

In this verse David is stuck on worrying about what somebody else is or isn't doing when he should be focused on what God is doing in him right now, in that cave! In his wonderful book *The Principle of the Path*, Andy Stanley says it this way: "Direction, not intention, determines our destination."[1]

I love those words and have had them pasted on my office vision board for years! Andy shares in life-changing detail how we can have all the passion for our future in the world, but if we don't keep our focus on Christ and keep moving—one step at a time toward Him, rather than being stuck in worry and comparison—we will miss our destiny.

I have heard *unstuck focus* being defined this way:

Fixed
On
Christ's
Unlimited
Supply
Every
Day

> Teach me your way, LORD . . . give me an undivided heart.
> (Ps. 86:11)

How Unstuck Focus Looks

Keep your eyes on God and be willing to give Him all of your heart, all of your soul, all of your strength, and all of your mind.

- When we have our *heart* focused on Him, we trust and lean on His Word.
- When we have our *soul* focused on Him, we keep our thoughts and our words in line with His thoughts and His words.
- When we have our *strength* focused on Him, we are counting on His abilities and not our own.
- When we have our *mind* focused on Him, we stay prepared to be amazed by what He does in us, through us, and in spite of us.

The second thing I see in this verse is *comparison*. Whether you see yourself as better or worse than another, my sweet sister, comparison is an evil tool of the enemy and it will keep you stuck faster than any other lie he tells you. As long as we stay wrapped up in comparison, isolated and separated from others, we are kept from the freedom God offers. A quote commonly attributed to C. S. Lewis puts it this way: "Humility is not thinking less of yourself, it's thinking of yourself less."

So, to remain unstuck, don't think of yourself as better or worse than someone else, or even pass yourself off as being ultra-humble . . . just think of yourself less and make much of God!

Don't Buy the Lie

The devil's goal is to divert your focus and isolate you to take you out. Remember, he is the master deceiver. When we are stuck comparing ourselves with and to others and are unwilling to take responsibility about where we go from here, we let our fears and weaknesses become our identity. When that happens, we accept lies about ourselves and God and we settle for survival in place of real life. We stay stuck in what we don't have instead of unstuck and able to take on all God has for us and the future He has planned for us.

Stuck focus can steal every morsel of joy from our lives, steal the glory God intended us to live in, and steal the intimacy God wants us to share with Him. That's why the deceiver, Satan, continually whispers lies about who we are, who God is, God's heart toward us, and the intimacy God wants us to share with Him. But by better understanding the devil's methods, we are better prepared to avoid his traps and enjoy unstuck focus. This is how it looks:

- **Strategic arrows are launched into our lives to create wounds:**
  difficult loss
  painful circumstances
  traumatic events
  neglect
  abuse

- **Our wounds become infected with lies or false beliefs and our focus goes the wrong direction:**
  "God has abandoned me too."
  "I'm a failure."
  "Nobody cares; it's up to me to look out for me."

- **Satan repeats lies until we make agreements to accept them as truth:**
  "I'm on my own now."
  "There's no hope."
  "I can't live without it."
  "This is all I deserve."

- **Once agreements are made, vows are soon to follow:**
  "I will never again . . . "
  "From now on, I will always . . . "

- **False agreements and vows feed the false self:**
  distorted views about who we are
  masks we wear to cover our true selves

●●●●●

It's little wonder Proverbs 4:23 instructs, "Above all else, guard your heart, for everything you do flows from it." The Lord clearly described how powerful the core beliefs of our hearts become in directing our lives and our legacies, echoed by Jesus throughout the New Testament. God is all about love, not hate. God is 100 percent invested in His love for us and in our love for others.

We find David a bit *stuck* here in this verse as through the words of Scripture we have the privilege of stepping into David's subconscious narrative (a bit unfair to David, I would say). We have had a front row seat into David's heart and emotions as he has uncovered, discovered, and processed God's "all-seeing eye" and boundless imagination. We were taken on a behind-the-scenes perspective of David's *peace with the past* and *purpose in his present*, and now we are taking hold, with David, of the power of *passion for the future*.

As David has truly wrapped his head and heart around his 3-D God, he enters his final struggle—*focus*. Remember, my friend, God delights in our differences. We are never, ever going to be the same thing, do the same thing, or experience success in the same ways as anyone else. God made us unique and special and with a particular purpose. But David begins *comparing*, saying, in essence, "God, you like me more because I like You more than they do. Let's 'totally' hate on them, God." Yikes!

Unstuck Friends

We women tend to stay stuck in the comparison trap. Sometimes, like David has done here, we allow ourselves to sit in judgment of one another: "If she would only . . ." "She really shouldn't . . ." "The reason she is suffering is because . . ." You get my drift, right? Honestly, friend . . . ugh. Don't we think it's time to stand together in this fight against the enemy instead of competing with one another?

Do you remember my husband's five words from Vietnam? I was so touched by his use of the word *brotherhood*. I love that. Can you imagine a time we need one another more than when we are in a hot fight with the enemy, splattered with mud, sweat, and tears? How about some *sisterhood* for us girls? Can I get an "amen"?

The thing is, her success is not your failure and her failure is not your success!

Even Winnie the Pooh gets this, telling us that "Good friends will stick with you until you're unstuck."[2] Here is how the Bible says it: "A friend loves at all times, and a brother is born for a time of adversity" (Prov. 17:17).

Perhaps David was a bit too familiar with a lack of trust. Bible scholars tell us that David probably wrote Psalm 139 while on the run from King Saul, possibly while hiding in a dark and scary cave. Not only that, consider the encounter with his brothers as he came upon the challenge of Goliath. Mind you, David's purpose for being there was to bring food to his brothers. David had already been identified as the future king by Samuel, but had then been sent back to the sheep fields. Sometimes God's assignments take far longer than we expect and we find ourselves in the places David found himself, waiting and wondering, *Did I make a mistake and God didn't really say that at all?*

> When Eliab, David's oldest brother, heard him speaking with the men, he burned with anger at him and asked, "Why have you come down here? And with whom did you leave those few sheep in the wilderness? I know how conceited you are and how wicked your heart is; you came down only to watch the battle." (1 Sam. 17:28)

The fact is, there are times when God is calling us to separate from the influence of certain friends and family. We must be very careful as well to evaluate those times.

Four Reasons to Go

Sometimes as we move on with God we are called to move away from certain friendships or relationships that cause us to falter. Other times we are to press through the challenges of a friendship and, as my dad would say, "take the bitter with the sweet." We definitely need to know when it is time to stick with a relationship or get unstuck so that God can do in us and through us what only He can do. It may be time to *let go* if:

1. *You feel you are stuck in an uphill battle.* When a relationship continues to drain everything you have to give without ever giving back, you may be stuck in enabling rather than real friendship.
2. *You are confronted with compromising situations over and over.* If you have been rescued from addiction, your addicted friends are not where you need to spend your time. You are not the Savior. You are only called to share what God has done in your life and offer Him as the answer. You cannot save your friends and family.
3. *You are only staying because you are stuck.* Are you stuck in fear, bad habits, insecurity, codependency, or obligation?
4. *The relationship is one-sided.* Your friend needs more than she gives. You are constantly the one on the giving side and never experience a feeling of mutual respect and value.

Four Reasons to Stay

However, it might be time to *hold on* if:

1. *This friend is supportive of who God created you to be.* She encourages you and spurs you on to all God intends for

your life without feeling threatened or held back in her own journey. She is growing and growing in God along with you.

2. *You have a common faith.* She speaks good words of faith and protects her thoughts. She pursues life unstuck along with you. She isn't a complainer, gossipy, negative, or fearful.

3. *She actually cares about you* and offers a balance of needing your support in day-to-day life along with giving hers. She demonstrates her love and friendship using her own spiritual gifts.

4. *She is a trusted accountability partner.* She lovingly spurs you toward repair when things get broken, and they do get broken. Instead of joining a crisis of belief, she can be counted on to hold you while you cry but drag you up out of bed when the season for tears has passed.

Remember, my friend, we all need one another; we need a network of mutual support, affection, loyalty, and encouragement. We need people we can be transparent with as we go through trials, who love us enough to help us keep our own focus and keep from getting stuck in the challenges of life.

23

UNSTUCK
Intimacy

Search me, God, and know my heart; test me and know my
anxious thoughts.

Psalm 139:23

When my daughter, Julianna, was about four or
five, she had some little girlfriends over to play
dress-up (yep, that same box my little Mikala
found many years later). In a moment of "mamma ignorance,"
or maybe sheer desperation, I left those little girls to take a quick
bath. I was barely bubbled up when Julianna pranced into the
bathroom, trailed by four little duckling girlfriends. I was horrified, not because I was lying in the bathtub naked, but because
Julianna and her little friends had faces covered with *blood red*
nail polish. All I could think of was, *Which is going to hurt worse,
calling their moms right now or sending them home rubbed raw
from nail polish remover? Geez, kids!*

It is an undeniable fact that girls like to dress up and have fun. We love to slip into that lacey dress and those glittering high heels for that special night out. But there are those times, those rare and special moments, when we don't want to be anything but *raw*. We want to wear baggy, ratty, fifteen-year-old sweatpants. We want to wad our hair up in a messy bun and go without makeup. We just want to be *free*.

Isn't it good to know that God loves no-frills us? He loves unmasked us. He loves unpolished us. He loves the you of the past, the you of the present, the you of the future.

As we head toward the finish line of our time together, I want to leave us with the sweet, sweet image of David's final surrender to the goodness of his Lord. To me, it is no accident, as nothing in God's Word is, that David ends these twenty-four verses in virtually the same place he started. The difference to me is intimacy.

Here, David declares in utter amazement how God searches and sees him inside and out: "O Lord, wow! You have searched me and know me. Me!" Here, I imagine a different tone in David's voice than we heard in the first verse. I hear a tone of hope, wonder, excitement, and surrender. I hear David relax.

"Search me, Lord! Test me," David says. "I know you've got something to show me, something to tell me, something to amaze me." I can almost hear one of my kids or "Gs" jumping up and down, saying, "Test me, G! See what I can do for you!"

Unstuck Truth #23: God breathes into me what He wants out of me!

Life unstuck hinges upon our face-to-face time with Jesus. Life unstuck is not lived on the shallow place of an "I'm a Christian and I go to church on Sunday," mentality. Life unstuck says, "I want the deep things of God. I want all God has for me. I want every single bit of intimate personal love that God had in mind when He created me to be me."

We all know what shallow relationships look like. We have "friends" on Facebook, Twitter, and Instagram, and we love those friends. Then we have close family and friends with whom we laugh and cry, and we do life with them. We work and we rest with them. But no matter how deep those relationships take us, Jesus has a deeper love. There is no one like the friend we have in Jesus. Just like with our fleshly friendships, an intimate, personal, growing relationship with Christ can only go as far as our face-to-face time allows. God wants our *more*.

> This is the confidence we have in approaching God: that if we ask anything according to his will, he hears us. And if we know he hears us—whatever we ask—we know that we have what we asked of him. (1 John 5:14–15)

Paul describes this place of *beholding* as the absolute center of the new covenant we have been brought into; the place where

> we all, with unveiled face, beholding as in a mirror the glory of the Lord, are being transformed into the same image from glory to glory, just as by the Spirit of the Lord. (2 Cor. 3:18 NKJV)

Intimacy doesn't result from performance for God but communing with Him. Only when we perceive the face of the One in whose image we were made do we come to know who we are and *whose* we are. When we take the time to sit in the presence of God, we are drawn into a place of intimacy that cannot be matched. The truth is that our intimate encounters with God reflect *directly* on our peace, purpose, and passion. The degree to which the Holy Spirit has freedom within us to do the transforming work of conforming us into the image of Christ will be the final determination of our life unstuck.

**Five Life-Changing Results
after Face-to-Face Encounters with God**

1. He discloses a heart not right with Him.
2. He will move heaven and earth on our behalf to move us from stuck to unstuck.
3. We exchange overwhelming odds for God-sized awesome.
4. His Word replaces sorrow and broken dreams with hope and wholeness.
5. His pure and holy presence provides unstuck peace, purpose, and passion.

This quest for His face is the *ultimate* quest.

Face-to-face encounters with God often look very different from one person to another. He reveals Himself to us, individually, according to His purposes. Sometimes, the way He chooses to reveal Himself is fully based upon what He sees hidden deep in our hearts. It is based upon our personal needs and level of desire to experience that revelation. It's impossible for us to live *unchanged* after such an encounter. Trading anything for more of God really is the greatest deal ever offered to mankind. What could I possibly have that would equal His value?

When God invades a person's life, things change. We watched David change over just the past twenty-three verses. I pray that we have changed with him . . . not only for ourselves, but also for the impact a life unstuck has on the rest of the world. The supernatural becomes natural when His glory is present. The things we used to work so hard for pale in the light of His presence. God's glory rests upon our lives following such divine encounters and affects every person we touch.

A heart to seek God is birthed in us by God Himself. Like all desires, it is not something that can be legislated or forced but

232

rather it grows within us as we become exposed to God's nature. He creates an appetite in us for Himself by lavishing upon us the reality of His goodness and His irresistible glory. God's love for people is beyond comprehension or imagination. He is *for* us, not against us; God is good *all* the time. These realities burn deeply into the hearts of all who simply take the time to press in close to Him.

How Do We Find Those Unstuck Encounters?

In his wonderful little book *Celebration of Discipline*, Richard Foster begins chapter 1 with this quote from Donald Coggan: "I go through life as a transient on his way to eternity, made in the image of God but with that image debased, needing to be taught how to meditate, to worship, to think." Foster then goes on to share this truth:

> Superficiality is the curse of our age. The doctrine of instant satisfaction is primarily a spiritual problem. The desperate need today is not for a greater number of intelligent people, or gifted people, but for deep people.[1]

Remember how I shared at the beginning of the book about 3-D women—dizzy, desperate, and digging? Life unstuck requires ordinary women—dizzy, desperate, and digging—to demand nothing less than extraordinary passion.

You have a choice!

Life unstuck on the outside. We must choose to be passionate about ordering our outside world to allow for what my friend Lysa TerKeurst calls "the best yes." In her words, "We have to slow the rhythm of the rush in our lives so the best of who we are can emerge."[2] Oh, yeah!

Life unstuck on the inside. We each wake up every single morning with the same number of hours in our day. We each wake up every single morning with the same opportunity no one can steal, to nourish our unseen life through chosen simplicity and devotional time (we *all* go to the bathroom, Mommy). It's like the discipline of the tithe; you will never know what the returns will be until you force yourself to obey God's instructions.

Life unstuck together. Life unstuck requires a fellowship of like-minded women, men, and families who come together to worship, study, and celebrate the awesomeness of God for and with one another. If you are singled out the enemy has an easy target.

You are possibly thinking *That all sounds good, but where do I start?* You start right where you are this very minute as you hold this book in your hands!

Unstuck Personality and Discipline

We have talked about how we shouldn't compare ourselves with one another, and that rule includes our intimacy with Jesus! Think back to chapter 3 where we talked about unstuck personalities and how God created each of us differently. He loves variety, and that includes how we interact with Him. In my early days as a believer, God connected me with the amazing and brilliant Florence Littauer and her daughters Marita and Lauren. Those ladies, along with others on the CLASS (Christian Leaders, Authors, and Speakers) staff, truly set me free in the ministry God called me into.

I learned the personality types that Florence captured—sanguine (butterfly), choleric (bumblebee), phlegmatic (ladybug), and melancholy (hummingbird), and incorporated them deeply into my family and ministry. I have always loved the truths I find in these revelations of how God so delicately crafted each of us. As I continued my study of the personality types both on business and personal levels, I ran into a little book by Tim LaHaye called *Spirit-Controlled Temperament* and another by his wife Beverly called *The*

Spirit-Controlled Woman. Both of these little books are dog-eared on my bookshelf. Unfortunately I can't share all about their books here, but I want to use my Garden of Personality to put my spin on their discoveries. We don't want to allow ourselves to get *stuck* in our inadequacies. We want a Spirit-filled life unstuck.

God is not surprised at you. He knows you. Let's take a look at these four examples and see where your personality type might struggle or shine in your desire to be more intimate with Jesus and more disciplined in your spiritual journey.

Butterfly Betsy

This "glass half full" sister is often found in life's overflow, as she loves to be part of everything and everyone. She sometimes just says yes to too much and finds her intimate time with Jesus taken up by too much other stuff. She is quick to volunteer, loves to dramatize, is often late, and is a bit lacking in the spiritual disciplines. God uses her strengths of transparency and love for people to minister to others who need her breath of fresh air.

Spiritual garden tip: have an accountability partner. Be creative about your place and time to sit with your Bible study, preferably with colorful notebooks, multicolored highlighting pens, a cup of hot tea, and a pretty napkin.

Hummingbird Hannah

Hannah will never be one to say yes without lots of consideration over the request to see how it fits in with her previous plans and commitments. Her first desire is to hear from the Holy Spirit as she takes on spiritual disciplines. She is artistic and gifted and often finds God through worshiping and the arts. She is well suited for in-depth study and biblical research. Call on her if you have a book or study to write!

Spiritual garden tip: step out of your comfort zone and join some friends in a time of morning prayer or a group study. Don't let all that study and those organized notes go to waste. Break out of your tendency to leave what God has shown you in your journal. Offer to lead a prayer group or a book study.

Bumblebee Barbara

Barbara usually has an abundance of confidence and can sometimes let the critical times of confession, surrender, and simply listening to God slip away in the skill of her take-charge leadership gifts. She is a good organizer and usually pretty faithful with her Bible study and journaling, but might need a ladybug buddy for allowing God to take her quiet time to places He wants her to go but she is not so sure of.

Spiritual garden tip: let someone else be the leader even though you may know more than her and be able to do it better. Watch for what God wants to show you. Allow God to surprise you and stir up your intimate times with Him. Look for His surprising moments of study and teaching.

Ladybug Lucy

Awwww, Lucy. You are so sweet at God's feet. You are dependable and consistent in your spiritual walk; just be careful not to get too complacent. You are gentle and patient but don't let yourself get lazy, sweet friend. Press into some fresh teaching. Allow God to go new places in your heart and soul, into your past and about your future.

Spiritual garden tip: challenge yourself to step into some unfamiliar places of intimacy with God. Do something that you wouldn't normally do, something outside your comfort zone, like raising your hands in worship or even dancing! Establish some specific goals for your personal time with God. Maybe read the Bible through in one year.

The bottom line: be yourself, but at the same time, challenge yourself to be your *best* unstuck self. Life unstuck comes from being passionate about giving our most treasured self to Jesus.

24

UNSTUCK
Life

See if there is any offensive way in me, and lead me in the way everlasting.

Psalm 139:24

Unstuck Dreams

"Mom, could you and Dad come over as soon as possible? I have something to show you." These words from my firstborn son immediately threw my imagination into action. What could he want to show us? I had my ideas! My son had been married with his own home for about two years when his phone call came. I had visions of a positive sign on an at-home pregnancy test, and had begun planning a citywide baby shower by the time we pulled into his driveway later that evening. As my husband and I pulled into the driveway, our son was standing in front of his open garage, literally beaming with joy.

"I knew it, I knew it!" I grabbed my husband's right arm from the steering wheel, causing him to barely miss the shrubbery that bordered the drive. "We are going to have a grandbaby! Oh my gosh!" We jumped out of the car and headed toward our son as he gestured toward the open garage door.

"Do you believe it?" he asked. "Can you believe my luck? Isn't she beautiful?" My eyes followed my son's gesture—and fell upon the ugliest, dirtiest old truck I had ever laid eyes on. It was from nineteen forty-something. I thought it looked like a piece of junk.

"Is this it? Is this what you wanted to show us?" I asked, drawing upon all of the motherly wisdom I could muster to not reveal my disappointment. The truck, nearly completely rusted away, had threadbare tires, cracked and filmy windows, torn and flaky seats, and came complete with the smell of old cigarettes. From my perspective, it was a lost cause.

"Yep, isn't it awesome?"

"What are you going to do with it, Tim?" I respectfully inquired.

"I am going to *restore* it!" he declared.

"Restore it, honey?"

"Yes, I am going to restore it. It will be so cool! I'm going to use a blowtorch to cut away all the old metal. I'm going to replace the old glass and rip out the torn seats. I'm going to paint her bright red, and before I am done she'll look brand-new and be worth a small fortune."

"But honey, what will you do with it then?" was my logical question.

"Mom," he proudly declared. "I am going to show it off to the world."

By the time my son was done sharing his vision for that old truck, both my husband and I could completely see his plan and had that brand-new truck fixed in our minds. That is exactly what God does with us, His girls! We come to God at various points in our lives, and to the world we may look a lot like that old truck.

We might seem a bit messed up, worn out, and even *stinky*. But God sees a different woman. He sees us as what we can be, if we allow Him to do the restoration that needs to be done. He sees us as a prized possession that, once redeemed, restored, and renewed, He will show off to the world—and everyone will know He has changed our lives.

When our son showed us that beat-up truck, he had a vision for what it would look like when he was finished with it and of the fun he would have showing it off. However, he had to start with what he had, and he knew he had work to do. We each have our own "condition," just like that old truck, to be considered. We saw in the very first verses of Psalm 139 that our thoughts, our actions, and our words matter to God. And as we close this journey through Psalm 139 together, I pray that these timeless words of David and these clumsy words of mine have awakened your vision for what God has for your unstuck life.

What's Your Dream?

OK, admit it! I'll bet you have seen and loved the movie *Pretty Woman*. It may be one of your secrets. I guess it should be one of mine. I know it doesn't have the most redeeming language or even a tad of biblical truth, but I do remember watching it long before knowing Jesus and even then thinking, *There is a dream for everyone; even the guy on the street knows that as he walks around Hollywood asking everyone who crossed his path, "What's your dream?"*

God designs every woman to give life, to give birth to, and to carry a dream, His dream, for her life. Just imagine, sister, God created you with a *dream* woven into your very center. He delicately and deliberately created and crafted you with a dream on your heart. To dream is to imagine, to form an idea or a wish in the imagination—in your heart. It is enlightening to research the word *imagine* and discover synonyms such as *aspire, perceive, wool gathering, imagination, daydream,* and even *stargaze.*

Do you know what your dreams are? God does! Remember, He is the God Who Sees. My prayer is that this book has caused you to take stock of your life—past, present, and future. Looking from God's eyes, what would you see? Would you see that beat-up old truck, or would you be able to see what Tim saw? Would you be able to see what God sees?

God has taken us on an amazing journey through Psalm 139. He has proven over and over how He wants His daughters unstuck in every way. He wants your dreams set free and your life unstuck!

How a Dream Leads Us to Life Unstuck

An Unstuck Dream Determines Our Direction to Destiny

Have you ever wondered what in the world your life is all about? *Is this all there is?* Are you that woman who secretly suspects there is nothing more but desperately dreams there is? An intentional God created every woman for intentional purposes. He had our entire life in mind, every single minute-hour-day, as He knit us together in our mother's womb. We don't have to be afraid of who God created us to be or the *huge* dreams, secret or spoken, He has planted in our hearts. A dream provides us with passion for life. Your dream may be to be a mother, or you may be a mother whose dreams right now are to just do it right! You may be completely invested in caring for a loved one or trapped in a painful medical diagnosis. You may be someone who is taking a risk and stepping into a dream today! Whatever you are doing right now, God put that dream in your heart. Remember Psalm 139:16, which reminds us *every day* is ordained before it comes to be. As God planted the dream, He planned the day.

An Unstuck Dream Gives Us Expectation and Confidence

When we have a dream, we can begin to see ourselves as God sees us. Along with the dream comes a new confidence in what we can accomplish with God's guidance and goodness. The bigger the dream, the bigger the God we need to make it come true. We have to trust God's ability to do in and with us what we cannot do outside of or without Him. "A blind man's world is bound by the limits of his touch; an ignorant man's world is bound by the limits of his knowledge; a great man's world by the limits of his vision."[1]

Let's dream a big dream for ourselves, girls—God does!

An Unstuck Dream Gives Us Boundaries That Keep Us Free

You do not have to tell a woman that there is much to get done and many people who need her to do it. We women are busy! However, as we mentioned earlier, we rarely, if ever, take time to focus on our own dreams and our own needs. A dream not only gives us direction toward our destination but also helps us to prioritize the present. A clear dream and plan we feel God has planted in us gives us the ability to "just say no" too. To know I can relinquish some of the many tasks someone else could capably do so that I can accomplish the one thing God has just for me to do gets me *unstuck*. A clear and articulated dream makes it easier to say yes and no.

An Unstuck Dream Leaves a Legacy

When we take a risk and go for the dream God plants in our heart, when we depend upon His provision, His direction, His protection, His anointing, and His love, we can do anything. When that "anything" is done—it will change the world!

History is full of examples of how this works, but let's look at this one. There was a woman by the name of Irene Sendler. During WWII she worked in a Warsaw ghetto as a plumber. She always knew God had a plan for her life, and dreamed of making a difference. When the Nazis began their destruction of the Jewish population, Irene decided *now* was her time. She began to smuggle babies out in the bottom of her toolbox, and carried larger children in the back of her truck under a burlap sack. She had a barking dog that scared the Nazi soldiers away and covered the noises from the crying babies. She smuggled out nearly 2,500 kids! She was eventually nominated for the Nobel Peace Prize. Talk about letting God work with where you are. *That* is passion, my friend.

Of course, we could go on and on throughout history until we get right here to you. After all, this is *all about you*. Now is the time for your unstuck passion and unstuck dreams to come true.

Look around you—there is an "old truck" somewhere that needs someone to see it shining and new.

Unstuck Truth #24: Life unstuck sees the invisible, believes the unbelievable, and receives the impossible.

Let's Dump Those Dream Stoppers

What are your dream stoppers? What prevents you from imagining big dreams or thinking beyond what your brain wants to "think" is possible? One common reason women do not embrace the dream that God has for us is that we do not truly understand who we belong to, who created us, or who we are in light of what Christ did on the cross for us. Yes, us! Me and you.

Some common dream stoppers are:

- You do not know or really *see* the God who sees you.
- Someone else has crushed your dreams and you cannot seem to get them back again.
- You are living in survivor mode, or "just trying to make it through today" mode.

243

- You believe that your dream is selfish or silly.
- You believe that you don't have what it takes. On your own, you don't—with God, you oh so do!
- You feel like it's too late or you don't have time.

It's time to dump that junk. Right now, today!

I love how James 4:7 says "yell a loud *no* to the Devil" (Message). Let's just say no to those lies, OK friend?

Christ went to the cross for you, sister—you are worthy of His dreams and your dreams. He delights in you. He created you just as you are. He sees you just as you are, knows all about you, and loves you. When we allow Him to, He gently uncovers those "dream stoppers" and then He restores our hearts and lives for His glory and our blessing. Do you want that? Do you want to trust God to do a makeover? To stir up a dream that soars beyond your greatest imagination?

The Bible says in Ephesians 2:10 that you are God's masterpiece. He created you to do good things. Good things are things you love to do. Ephesians 3:20 says God is able to do immeasurably more than we can ask or imagine. Wow. I can imagine so much! Take some time to dream, my friend.

What might God be calling you to do?

What might He be calling you to say?

What dreams have you had on hold that need to be unstuck?

What "more than you can imagine" might God have in store for you?

Ask Him! He wants to tell you and it is time for you to take the next step to an unstuck dream. What is that step? God wants to use us to change the world. He wants to use our past, our present, and our future. He wants to use our gifts and talents, to redirect our weaknesses and heal our broken hearts. He wants to challenge our safe places because He wants to be our safe place. Remember, life unstuck begins at the end of our comfort zone! This is how the world is changed.

As we arrive at the end of this journey, I am going to miss you, that face I have had in my mind's eye as I have written and given all I have to these pages—for better or worse. You see, you are holding a dream of mine, right here in your tender hands. And if you are reading these words, you have actually read the whole thing. I am breathless with thanksgiving.

I am a woman just like you, who tends to wake up, day to day, sometimes stuck and sometimes unstuck.

God has blessed me with peace with my past but sometimes I run headfirst into a leftover loss. He has clearly revealed His purpose and calling on my life to share His love and hope with women, but sometimes I feel loveless and hopeless. I have dishes in the sink from last night and dirty laundry still piled up from the weekend. I have a husband and family who need and want my "part" in their lives. God has placed passion in my heart for tomorrow and reminds me of the "more than I can imagine" He says He can do, but sometimes I just can't imagine. I know you join me in the passionate desire to live life unstuck so that Jesus can shine through us!

Life unstuck is an ordinary journey with an extraordinary God.

God knows your heart, my darling friend. He knows your dreams just like He knows mine. And someday you will see that unstuck dream come to life. Someday you *will* touch it with your hands like you are touching this book.

You are a one-of-a-kind unique design; live like you believe it!

. . . .

I would be so honored to hear about your dream! Join me at life -unstuck.com. We need one another!

Acknowledgments

ow could any kind of acknowledgment for this book not begin with the love of my life—my husband, Mike, aka "Honey" and/or "My Marine." You, my amazing husband, have been "the wind beneath my wings" as they say and the closest I will ever come on this earth to an amazing-grace love that has stood the test of time. Thank you for walking every single page of this journey with me. You may now do a happy dance (as long as no one else sees you!). It is done.

To our three adult children Tim, Andy, and Julianna; two awe-some "daughters-in-love" Kim and Bethany; and five *grand*children AJ, Jacob, Mikala, Kai, and Bella. You will all see your names on the pages of this book. We have been challenged, we have been blessed, we have been stuck and unstuck. If I could have brain-stormed with God and designed my own family—you would be exactly who you are. I love you.

As I have written the words in this book, one word in particular has wrapped around my shoulders like a treasured blanket—that word is *family*. I am honored to take this moment in time to claim Psalm 139:13 and thank God for my mom, in whose womb He chose for me to be knit together. For my sisters, Pam, Peggy, and Paula, who share that blessing: I love you and I am grateful for God's choice for me. For us.

Many years ago, as I started my walk with the Lord, I picked up a little book called *Breaking Free* by an emerging Christian author named Beth Moore. I have met you a few times in the flesh, but you "met me" on the pages of *Breaking Free*. Thank you, Beth, for saying yes to God. Every tiny morsel of ministry and freedom I have to share started through your challenge to believe God's precious and redeeming truth for my life.

To Lysa TerKeurst, my precious "little spiritual sister." This book is in someone's hands, with the title it has on the cover, because of you. Your friendship and sacrificial coaching through COMPEL have absolutely changed my life. Serving with you, the staff, and the board at Proverbs 31 Ministries (www.proverbs31 .org) is one of the sweetest honors of my life.

To my editor, Kim Bangs, my writing researcher, Melissa Loudermilk, and my agent, DJ Snell: "Thank you" just ain't enough. (Did that make the cut?) Snuggled right next to my desire to honor Jesus is the fact that I want to make you proud of putting so much effort into me. I am hard work, right? Thank you for taking the job!

Notes

Chapter 2 Unstuck Thoughts

1. Priscilla Shirer, *The Resolution for Women* (Nashville: B&H, 2011), 123.
2. Oswald Chambers, "Do It Yourself," *My Utmost for His Highest* (repr., Uhrichsville, OH: Barbour, 2000), 182.

Chapter 3 Unstuck Personality

1. Vonette Bright, *The Woman Within: Discover the Woman God Made You to Be* (Wheaton: Tyndale, 2004), xviii.
2. For more information about Florence Littauer and her work with personality types, see her book *Personality Plus* (Grand Rapids: Revell, 1992).

Chapter 4 Unstuck Chick Chatter

1. Charles H. Spurgeon, "Psalm 139:4," *The Treasury of David*, accessed August 20, 2014, http://www.biblestudytools.com/commentaries/treasury-of-david/psalms-139-4.html.

Chapter 7 Unstuck Peace

1. John Trent, *LifeMapping: A Helpful, Hands-On Process for Overcoming Your Past, Taking Control of Your Present, and Charting Your Future* (New York: Doubleday, 1998), 36.
2. H. Norman Wright, *Making Peace with Your Past* (Grand Rapids: Revell, 1984), 9.
3. Nancy Rue and Rebecca St. James, *The Merciful Scar* (Nashville: Thomas Nelson, 2013), 284.
4. A. W. Tozer, *The Pursuit of God* definitive classic edition (Ventura, CA: Regal, 2013), 19.

Chapter 10 Unstuck Freedom

1. Patricia Layton, *A Surrendered Life: A Thoughtful Approach to Finding Freedom, Healing and Hope after Abortion* (Grand Rapids: Baker, 2014), 70.

Chapter 12 Unstuck Vision

1. Adapted from "Juliette Gordon Low Biography," Girl Scouts, accessed August 21, 2014, http://www.girlscouts.org/who_we_are/history/low_biography/.

Chapter 13 Unstuck Purpose

1. Jack Frost, "4 Keys to Restoring Intimacy with God," *CharismaNews*, January 11, 2014, http://www.charismanews.com/opinion/42317-4-keys-to-restoring -intimacy-with-god?showall=&start=1.

Chapter 14 Unstuck Praise

1. Mark Pygas, "40 Astounding Facts You Should Know About Your Amazing Human Body," accessed September 10, 2014, http://news.distractify.com/dark/ trivial-facts/amazing-facts-about-the-human-body/.
2. Betsey Stevenson and Justin Wolfers, "The Paradox of Declining Female Happiness," NBER Working Paper No. 14969, May 2009, http://www.nber.org/ papers/w14969.

Chapter 16 Unstuck Surprises

1. Bureau of Labor Statistics, "Charts from the American Time Use Survey," *American Time Use Survey*, accessed September 12, 2014, http://www.bls.gov/ tus/charts/.
2. Michael Hyatt, "The Perfect Moment," *Michael Hyatt*, February 18, 2008, http://michaelhyatt.com/the-perfect-moment.html.

Chapter 18 Unstuck Rest

1. Jill Briscoe, *The Deep Place Where Nobody Goes: Conversations with God on the Steps of My Soul* (Oxford: Monarch, 2005), 17.
2. Lysa TerKeurst, *The Best Yes: Making Wise Decisions in the Midst of Endless Demands* (Nashville: Thomas Nelson, 2014), 236.

Chapter 19 Unstuck Passion

1. Charles Spurgeon, "Psalm 139:19," *The Treasury of David*, accessed September 10, 2014, http://www.biblestudytools.com/commentaries/treasury-of-david/ psalms-139-19.html.
2. TerKeurst, *The Best Yes*, 89.

Chapter 20 Unstuck Woman Warrior

1. Beth Moore, *Breaking Free: Making Liberty in Christ a Reality in Life* (Nashville: Lifeway, 2002), 3.

Chapter 21 Unstuck Emotions

1. Gary Chapman and Jennifer Thomas, *The Five Languages of Apology: How to Experience Healing in All Your Relationships* (Chicago: Northfield, 2008).
2. Ibid., 62.

Chapter 22 Unstuck Focus

1. Andy Stanley, *The Principle of the Path: How to Get from Where You Are to Where You Want to Be* (Nashville: Thomas Nelson, 2011), 14.
2. As quoted in "Disney On: Friendship," *Oh My Disney*, August 11, 2014, http://blogs.disney.com/oh-my-disney/2014/08/07/disney-on-friendship/.

Chapter 23 Unstuck Intimacy

1. Richard Foster, *Celebration of Discipline: The Path to Spiritual Growth* (San Francisco: Harper San Francisco, 1998), 1.
2. Lysa TerKeurst, "It's Almost Here . . . The Best Yes," LysaTerKeurst.com, July 5, 2014, http://lysaterkeurst.com/2014/07/its-almost-here-the-best-yes/.

Chapter 24 Unstuck Life

1. E. Paul Hovey, "E. Paul Hovey Quotes," Good Reads, accessed August 19, 2014, https://www.goodreads.com/author/quotes/1096675.E_Paul_Hovey.

Pat Layton, wife of thirty-seven years, mom of three, mother in "love" of two beautiful young women, and "G" (grandmother) of five, is a passionate and inspiring leader who during her twenty-five years in full-time ministry has founded a variety of nonprofit ministries including a pregnancy resource center (A Woman's Place Ministries), a Christian adoption agency (The Woven Basket), and an abstinence education program (Impact). Pat currently serves as founder and president of an international ministry called Living Free, which hosts a national woman's conference called Imagine Me . . . Redeemed, Restored, Renewed . . . Set Free, and an international post-abortion recovery program called Surrendering the Secret. Pat serves on the board of directors of Proverbs 31 Ministries and is a busy speaker, author, and life coach specializing in "dream design" for women. Her other books include *A Surrendered Life*, the post-abortion recovery Bible study *Surrendering the Secret*, and a Bible study gift book series called Born to Bloom. Pat and her husband, Mike, have been a part of Grace Family Church in Tampa, Florida, for over twenty years and serve as elders.

Every spare moment that is not filled with "all of the above" is stolen for rocking on her front porch drinking sweet tea and reading a decorating magazine. You can join Pat in the adventure of faith at www.patlayton.net, where she shares it all, including the sweet tea!

. . . .

Join the Unstuck Woman Club! Please visit our website today at life-unstuck.com for free prizes and giveaways. Join lots of other women as we work our way from dizzy, desperate, and digging to life unstuck! We will share insights, advice, and mutual struggles over marriage, family, finances, ministry, calling, and cellulite. Please join us today and say hello for a free gift!

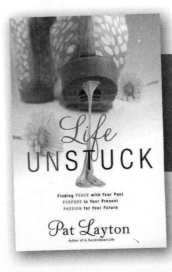

Proverbs 31
MINISTRIES

If you were inspired by *Life Unstuck* and desire to deepen your own personal relationship with Jesus Christ, I encourage you to connect with Proverbs 31 Ministries.

Proverbs 31 Ministries exists to be a trusted friend who will take you by the hand and walk by your side, leading you one step closer to the heart of God through:

- ❋ Free online daily devotions
- ❋ Daily radio program
- ❋ Books and resources
- ❋ Online Bible studies
- ❋ COMPEL writer's training:
  WWW.COMPELTRAINING.COM

To learn more about Proverbs 31 Ministries call **877-731-4663** or visit **www.Proverbs31.org**.

Proverbs 31 Ministries
630 Team Rd., Suite 100
Matthews, NC 28105
www.Proverbs31.org

FREEDOM, HEALING, and **HOPE**

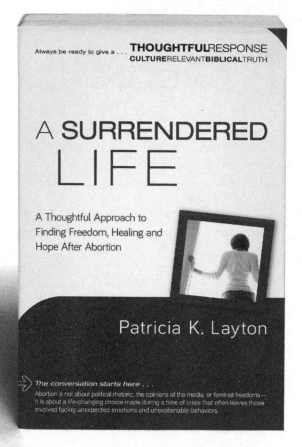

Always be ready to give a . . . **THOUGHTFUL**RESPONSE **CULTURE**RELEVANT**BIBLICAL**TRUTH

A **SURRENDERED** LIFE

A Thoughtful Approach to Finding Freedom, Healing and Hope After Abortion

Patricia K. Layton

The conversation starts here . . .

Abortion is not about political rhetoric, the opinions of the media, or feminist freedoms—it is about a life-changing choice made during a time of crisis that often leaves those involved facing unexpected emotions and unexplainable behaviors.

More than 40 percent of women in their childbearing years have had an abortion. Through her own story and the stories of others, Pat Layton guides women on a faith-based journey toward emotional and spiritual healing.

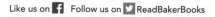